Praise for
The Principal's Handbook for Leading Inclusive Schools

"A fine contribution to the professional literature on inclusive schools, this book provides . . . practical, research-based information on a range of nuts and bolts topics related to developing and supporting an inclusive school."
—**James McLeskey, Ph.D.,** Professor, School of Special Education, School Psychology, and Early Childhood Studies, College of Education, University of Florida

"Finally! A book for administrators outlining both the values and the practices of inclusive schools. It is current. It is visionary. Above all, it is inspiring. This book should be on the desktop of every school leader."
—**Paula Kluth, Ph.D.,** author, *"You're Going to Love This Kid!"*

"Masterful in its directness and simplicity, this book captures the essentials of principal leadership. . . . These authors created a text that speaks WITH principals, not AT them."
—**Michael McSheehan,** Clinical Assistant Professor, Communication Sciences and Disorders, Project Director, National Center on Inclusive Education, University of New Hampshire

"If there is ever a school administrator seeking advice on creating a culture of effective inclusive practice, this book has the answers!"
—**Carol Quirk, Ed.D.,** Co-Executive Director, Maryland Coalition for Inclusive Education

"A straightforward, realistic, and empowering guide that will help principals move their school culture from one of 'doing inclusion' to inclusive."
—**Linda K. Llewellyn,** Director of Instruction, Homer Central School District

The Principal's Handbook
for Leading Inclusive Schools

The Principal's Handbook
for Leading Inclusive Schools

by

Julie Causton, Ph.D.
Syracuse University

and

George Theoharis, Ph.D.
Syracuse University

·P A U L·H·
BROOKES
PUBLISHING C^o. ®

Baltimore • London • Sydney

Paul H. Brookes Publishing Co.
Post Office Box 10624
Baltimore, Maryland 21285-0624
USA

www.brookespublishing.com

Typeset by Apex CoVantage, LLC, Herndon, Virginia.
Manufactured in the United States of America by
Sheridan Books, Inc., Chelsea, Michigan.

Cover image ©istockphoto/littleclie

Author photos on page vii provided by Syracuse University.

The cartoons that appear at the beginning of each chapter are reprinted by permission from Giangreco, M.F. (2007). *Absurdities and realities of special education: The complete digital set [CD]*. Thousand Oaks, CA: Corwin Press.

Portions of this book were previously published in *The Paraprofessional's Handbook for Effective Support in Inclusive Classrooms* by Julie Causton-Theoharis, Copyright © 2009 Paul H. Brookes Publishing Co., Inc. All rights reserved.

Library of Congress Cataloging-in-Publication Data
Causton, Julie.
    The principal's handbook for leading inclusive schools / by Julie Causton, Ph.D. and George
    Theoharis, Ph.D.
        pages   cm
    Includes bibliographical references and index.
    ISBN 978-1-59857-298-8 (pbk.) — ISBN 1-59857-298-9 (pbk.)
    1. Inclusive education—United States.   2. Mainstreaming in education—United States.
    3. Special education—United States.   4. School administrators—United States—Handbooks,
    manuals, etc.   5. School principals—United States—Handbooks, manuals, etc.   I. Title.
    LC1201.C375   2013
    371.9'046—dc23   2013016809

British Library Cataloguing in Publication data are available from the British Library.

2017   2016   2015   2014   2013

10   9   8   7   6   5   4   3   2   1

Contents

About the Forms

Purchasers of this book may download, print, and/or photocopy the blank forms for educational use. These materials are included with the print book and are also available at **http://www.brookespublishing.com/causton/eforms** for both print and e-book buyers.

About the Authors

Julie Causton, Ph.D., is an expert in creating and maintaining inclusive schools. She is Associate Professor in the Inclusive and Special Education Program, Department of Teaching and Leadership, Syracuse University. She teaches courses on inclusion, differentiation, special education law, and collaboration. Her published works have appeared in such journals as *Behavioral Disorders, Equity & Excellence in Education, Exceptional Children, International Journal of Inclusive Education, Journal of Research in Childhood Education, Studies in Art Education,* and *TEACHING Exceptional Children.* Julie also works with families, schools, and districts directly to help to create truly inclusive schools. She co-directs a summer leadership institute for school administrators focusing on issues of equity and inclusion as well as a school reform project called Schools of Promise. Her doctorate in special education is from the University of Wisconsin–Madison.

George Theoharis, Ph.D., is Associate Dean in the School of Education and Associate Professor in Educational Leadership and Inclusive Elementary Education in the Department of Teaching and Leadership, Syracuse University. He has extensive field experience in public education as a principal and as a teacher. George teaches classes in educational leadership and elementary/early childhood teacher education. His interests, research, and work with K–12 schools focus on issues of equity, justice, diversity, inclusion, leadership, and school reform. His book *The School Leaders Our Children Deserve* (Teachers College Press, 2009) is about school leadership, social justice, and school reform. He is co-editor of a new book *What Every Principal Needs to Know*

to Create Excellent and Equitable Schools (Teachers College Press, 2013). George's published works appear in such journals as *Educational Administration Quarterly, Educational Leadership, Equity & Excellence in Education, International Journal of Inclusive Education, Journal of School Leadership, Journal of Special Education Leadership, Remedial and Special Education, The School Administrator, Teachers College Record,* and *Urban Education.* He co-runs a summer leadership institute for school administrators focusing on issues of equity and inclusion as well as a school reform project called Schools of Promise. His doctorate in educational leadership and policy analysis is from the University of Wisconsin–Madison.

Foreword

I am pleased to write the foreword for this book, as the attitudes, dispositions, and skills possessed by the primary audience for this book (i.e., school principals) determine whether or not doors are opened and opportunities provided for students or doors are closed and options, opportunities, and choices are denied. This valuable text provides information that should help to develop attitudes, dispositions, and skills on the part of school leaders that will forward inclusive education.

THE PAST

When asked to write the foreword to *The Principal's Handbook for Leading Inclusive Schools* by Julie Causton and George Theoharis, I immediately began to reflect upon my own journey as a school leader trying to facilitate the creation of an inclusive school community. A vivid memory from 1984 popped into my head. My wife and colleague Jacque Thousand and I were asked to deliver an hour and a half in-service to a group of administrators on the topic of inclusion. At the time, Jacque was Assistant Professor at the University of Vermont and coordinator of the Homecoming Project, the first federally funded model demonstration project to show how students with severe disabilities could successfully be educated in general education classrooms in neighborhood schools. I was working as an administrator in the Winooski, Vermont, school district, one of the nation's first fully inclusive schools and a participant district in the Homecoming Project. I recall how flattered we were to have been asked to present and wondering if we even had enough content to fill an hour and a half. We prepared our overheads and slides for our presentation and traveled to southern Vermont where we delivered the in-service training.

That evening, feeling pleased that we had been well received by the audience, we shared with each other our amusement and amazement about the fact that someone was actually paying us to come and talk to them about what we perceived to be pure common sense. We were sure that the social justice values that underpin inclusion, along with the emerging organizational and instructional practices that make inclusion successful for students with and without disabilities in mixed-ability classrooms, and the dispositions of creativity and collaboration essential to crafting personalized and differentiated supports, would quickly be recognized and adopted by most to all school districts. Oh, the optimism of youth! We learned soon afterward and have been reminded periodically over the past 30 years that what we perceive to be common sense still is not the vision or practice in way too many school communities.

THE PRESENT

The good news is that since the time of our first presentation on inclusive education, there has been a steady trend toward more inclusion. Further, much has been learned about the variables that need to be in place to ensure that what is created in the name of inclusion becomes a good example of a good practice rather than a bad example of a good practice. In other words, there is more common sense available today than when the first demonstrations of inclusion were launched. We now can fill weeks rather than hours of professional development in the organizational and instructional practices that make inclusion work.

Although much has been and continues to be learned, it is important to point out that many of the fundamental variables essential to making inclusion successful in 1984 remain to be essential today. The role of the school principal is a perfect example. We have long known that the principal is essential to the success of any major reform initiative in a school. A policy study conducted in multiple states on least restrictive environment and inclusion (Hasazi, Johnston, Liggett, & Schattman, 1994) concluded that how the building principal at each school site chose to view the issue determined whether anything changed at that school. Similar findings were found in a study we conducted in inclusive schools in five states and one Canadian province (Villa, Thousand, Meyers, & Nevin, 1996). The study identified three variables as most highly correlated with a positive attitude by general and special educators toward inclusion: 1) the degree of administrative support for the practice, 2) collaboration, and 3) experience.

Another learning about leadership and system change in schools that has remained constant across my years of work assisting schools and school districts in the United States and other countries to transform systems to be inclusive is that change and progress in education requires school leaders to attend to five elements of a systems change formula. These five elements are vision, skills, incentives, resources, and action planning. First, school leaders must build a *vision* based on the assumptions that 1) all students are capable of learning, 2) all students have a right to an education with their peers in their community's schools, 3) everyone who provides instruction shares responsibility for the learning of every student in the school, and 4) inclusive practices benefit all students and educators alike. In addition, school leaders must develop educators' *skills* and confidence to educate students in mixed-ability classrooms; create meaningful *incentives* for people to take the risk to embark on an inclusion journey; reorganize, schedule, and expand human and other *resources*; and plan for and take *actions* designed to get school personnel excited about implementing inclusive practices. Julie Causton and George Theoharis have crafted an excellent book filled with chapters that instruct principals on how to do all of the above. They skillfully

1. Clarify the *vision* of an inclusive school and address the role of the school principal in shepherding this vision
2. Provide information and strategies that add to the readers' conceptual, technical, and interpersonal *skill* set
3. Illustrate the importance of collaborative and creative processes, identify *incentives* (e.g., training in differentiation and co-teaching, scheduling, the use of a strength-based perspective when exploring the mismatch between the facts about a learner and the classroom environment and demands)
4. Address allocation and reallocation of *resources*, coordination of initiatives
5. Provide the reader with the necessary information to craft an *action plan* for creating an inclusive school

THE FUTURE

I may be older than when I began this journey but I am no less optimistic. It is my sincere belief that this book will motivate and empower you, the reader, to move forward so that through your learning, efforts, and actions common sense finally becomes common and attainable in all of our nation's schools. In the words of W.H. Murray,

> Until one is committed there is hesitancy, the chance to draw back, always ineffectiveness. Concerning all acts of initiative . . . there is one elementary truth, the ignorance of which kills countless ideas and splendid plans: That the moment one definitely commits oneself, then providence moves too. (as quoted in Gore, 1992, p. 16)

The future belongs to those who lead. The students and the future await your inspired and informed leadership.

Richard A. Villa, Ed.D.
Bayridge Consortium, Inc.
San Diego, California

REFERENCES

Gore, A. (1992). *Earth in the balance: Ecology and the human spirit.* Boston, MA: Houghton Mifflin.

Hasazi, S., Johnston, R, Liggett, A., & Schattman, R. (1994). A qualitative policy study of the least restrictive environment provision of the Individuals with Disabilities Education Act. *Exceptional Children, 60,* 491–507.

Villa, R.A., Thousand, J.S., Meyers, H., & Nevin, A. (1996). Teacher and administrator perceptions of heterogenous education. *Exceptional Children, 63*(1), 29–45.

Preface

Inclusive Schooling Requires Leadership

This book comes out of very personal work. When George first became a principal, he entered a school that had isolated pockets of inclusion, maintained a self-contained program for students with significant needs, and had a tradition of pulling students out for all kinds of educational needs and therapies, including special education, speech-language pathology, English as a second language (ESL), occupational therapy, physical therapy, remedial reading, and so forth. Students were coming and going from classrooms and teachers were working very hard, but the students with the most needs had disjointed programs and were marginal school community members due to their transitions or self-contained programs.

Teachers did not have time to co-plan or collaborate, and the result was a frustrated staff and declining student achievement. There was overrepresentation of students of color and low-income students receiving special education services at the school. A disproportionate number of students of color and low-income students with disabilities received instruction outside of the general education classroom and the *vast* majority of behavioral and discipline referrals were students of color and low-income students with disabilities.

George led the staff in planning for collaborative and inclusive services for students with disabilities but also as a schoolwide philosophy that extended to all services, such as ESL, remedial reading, and academic enrichment. The result was a school that had teams of professionals that collaborated to co-plan and co-deliver instruction in inclusive ways. All instruction and the vast majority of therapies were integrated and co-delivered in the general education classroom. This changed the ways teachers and therapists did their jobs. It is important to note that pullout services were not replaced by pulling students with disabilities to the table in the back of the general education classroom, but that general education teachers, special education teachers, and therapists co-planned instruction and accommodations.

The results were an improved climate in the school, a reduction of discipline issues, a lower special education placement rate, and significant gains in student achievement for all students across all demographic groups—including students with disabilities. This was not a utopian school but a regular place. Some teams worked better than others, some teachers believed wholeheartedly that inclusive services were best, and some had serious reservations. Leadership was key—leadership by the principal as well as a leadership team that made key decisions maintained the focus on collaborative inclusive services. The leadership team was made up of representatives from each team or grade level, who were chosen by their colleagues.

George's role as school principal was essential to moving the school in a more inclusive direction. It involved carrying the torch of an inclusive vision, leading the charge in service delivery, creating and developing teams, and providing support (planning time, space, and materials) for teams to co-plan and co-teach.

Since the late 1990s, Julie has been working alongside, coaching, prodding, and supporting principals as they do the work of creating and maintaining inclusive schools. Not only has she helped them think strategically about the work of supporting their staff to create the schools of their dreams, but she also provided professional development to those teachers and paraprofessionals and therapists to help them reenvision their service delivery models.

She has held their hands in the face of adversity and staff discontent and helped them to step up and lead their schools to become more inclusive spaces. As in George's school, the results have been schools and districts that no longer segregate and separate but instead embrace *all* students as part of the academic and social community. Academic achievement gains were made for students with and without disabilities in all cases, and the teachers know how to collaborate and co-design effective inclusive units and lessons. Climate has improved, and most important, all students feel a stronger sense of belonging, as their membership is no longer in question.

We have worked with and studied a great many school leaders who have engaged in this work. This work has informed and shaped many of the specifics in this book. It has also confirmed what we knew: that inclusive schools require strong, committed, knowledgeable, and visionary inclusive leaders.

ON INCLUSION

Not a day goes by when we don't think about inclusion. When we both think of the amazing students and staff we have had the privilege of teaching and leading, we are reminded of what *teachers and leaders* they were to us. They have taught us that everyone has a right to belong, to have friends, to have access to engaging curricula, and to have powerful instruction. Everyone has a right to be treated with dignity and with gentle, respectful support, and to experience that learning is intimately connected with feeling like part of the classroom. Every student deserves to receive support in a warm and welcoming place. The more this happens, the more we have created the environment for substantial learning. It isn't, therefore, just about creating a sense of belonging for belonging's sake; that sense of connection and welcome paves the way for academic and social growth. We know that if inclusion is to be a schoolwide reality, leadership is required. Therefore, this book is designed as a guide for principals and school leaders as they work to include all students with disabilities in gentle, respectful, and meaningful ways.

HOW THIS BOOK IS ORGANIZED

The first three chapters provide the context for the rest of the book: Chapter 1 focuses on the role of the principal or school leader, Chapter 2 provides background about special education, and Chapter 3 provides information about inclusive education. These first chapters provide the foundation necessary to more effectively interpret the rest of the book. Chapter 4 provides leaders with strategies to move beyond pockets of inclusion. This chapter lays out a process and tools to help leaders engage in inclusive school reform. Chapter 5 is about leading effective collaboration—the backbone of inclusive schools. In Chapter 6, we ask leaders to look at students through the lens of strengths and abilities—to reconsider some of the negative descriptors—for the sake of being able to reach and support all students more effectively. Chapters 7 and 8 are strategy-specific chapters that focus on academic supports and behavioral supports. These strategy-specific chapters provide ideas that are immediately applicable in schools. The last chapter focuses on self-care and problem solving. The job of including students in our school systems who pose the greatest challenges and require the most complex problem solving is not an easy one, and we recognize the toll that this can have on school leaders. Chapter 9 is meant to give helpful ideas for how leaders can care for themselves in order to provide the best possible education for students.

WHO WILL FIND THIS BOOK USEFUL?

As more and more schools move toward inclusive education, principals and other school leaders are the most critical factor to success. The role of the school leader is changing, and this book represents cutting-edge ideas and strategies to create and maintain authentic inclusive schools. The idea of the principal as critical to inclusion disrupts traditional thinking in two ways: First, it allows us to move beyond islands of inclusion in only certain classrooms and toward inclusive schools—positioning the principal as central to taking up that charge—and second, we move beyond the idea that it is okay to include some but maintain outdated and ineffective pullout and self-contained programs. Leaders are essential in the work of doing inclusion well. They need to be the champions of a vision of inclusion and the effective managers to make the realities of inclusion a priority. Conversely, without appropriate knowledge or support, leaders can disrupt the inclusion of students with disabilities by following the traditional "remove and remediate" philosophy. That being said, a team approach to supporting students in the classroom is necessary. Although this book will primarily serve principals who want to learn more about creating and maintaining authentic inclusive schools, it is critical that this book is read by the directors of special education, special educators, general educators, other administrators, parents, and other schools leaders who are team players in supporting students in inclusive school communities.

Practicing and preservice school leaders: This book is written specifically for practicing leaders working in or hoping to work in inclusive schools in K–12 settings. However, this book is also perfect for students in educational leadership programs at colleges and universities.

Special educators, including related service providers: Special educators support students in inclusive classrooms. This book identifies approaches, strategies, and suggestions for supporting all students in inclusive classrooms. This book can be used for leaders and special educators to read and discuss together in a professional development or book club format.

General educators: General educators are an important part of the classroom team. Learning more about inclusive leadership allows general educators to offer a seamless and thoughtful integration of services.

Parents of students with special needs: Parents can benefit from this book by understanding the best practices for inclusive school leadership. For them, this book can be a resource to secure help to create inclusive schools beyond just isolated inclusive classrooms.

Professional development personnel: This book offers cutting-edge approaches and resources for any principal training or leadership development.

This book is intended as a companion guide to *The Paraprofessional's Handbook for Effective Support in Inclusive Classrooms* (Paul H. Brookes Publishing Co., 2009) so that educational teams can gain shared knowledge. It is purposefully organized in the same way, using the same headings and much of the same information, shared from a very different perspective and point of view. We are currently in the process of writing several more handbooks and hope to see all of these books used together as teams work collaboratively to support all students in inclusive settings.

Acknowledgments

JULIE'S ACKNOWLEDGMENTS

This book is about leadership—thoughtful, imaginative, forward thinking, passionate leadership—that allows people to reach their full potential, become their best selves, and do their best work. This work is a call for a different paradigm in schools, one in which support is available for all to create the community essential for learning. And this work is driven by a vision of substantive and meaningful inclusion for *all* children.

Indeed, this book and my own academic career would not have been possible without all sorts of leadership. Therefore, I feel it is necessary to thank the sizeable community of students, teachers, scholars, family, and friends who have led me in both visible and invisible ways as we have written this book. I want to thank the many individuals who have helped me see the importance of the journey, imagine the route, and stay the course.

To my students: I have worked with many students over the years, and each taught me something new. I would especially like to thank those who have forced me to think in new ways: Chelsea, Joryann, Ricki, Josh, Moua, Brett, Shawnee, Adam, Trevor, and Gabe.

To my teaching partner: Kathie Crandall, my friend, who taught me that laughter is truly the best indicator of learning.

To my teachers: Lou Brown, whose belief in inclusion has inspired me throughout my entire academic career, and Alice Udvari-Solner, who has sustained me with her intellectual vision, creativity, and commitment to *all* children. Your work has touched every aspect of this book, and it is impossible to say where your influence ends. I also thank Kimber Malmgren and Colleen Capper, whose mentorship has made my career in education possible.

To my friends and colleagues: Chelsea Tracy-Bronson, Christy Ashby, Sharon Dotger, Paula Kluth, Patrick Schwarz, Michael Giangreco, Doug Biklen, Corrine Roth Smith, Beth Ferri, Thomas Bull, Corrie Burdick, Meghan Cosier, Tara Affolter, and Steve Hoffman: You help me through each and every day and remind me that there is much more to life than work. And to George Theoharis: Thank you for being an exceptional co-parent and creative and thoughtful colleague.

To Paul H. Brookes Publishing Co.: I thank Rebecca Lazo, Steve Plocher, and all of the Brookes staff for your helpful suggestions and creative vision.

To Stephanie Perotti: You brighten my days and bring an enthusiasm and energy to my life that is unparalleled. Thank you!

To my family: Ella Theoharis and Sam Theoharis, you make me laugh every day and inspire me to make the world of schooling better for you and all children. You are the biggest blessing in my life! Thanks to Gail Andre, Jeff Causton, and Kristine Causton for being excited about the importance of my work.

GEORGE'S ACKNOWLEDGMENTS

This book is about leadership to create more inclusive, and therefore more socially just, schools. We know that this leadership is not the work of a "heroic" individual working alone. This requires a variety of people to play leadership roles from various positions in the school community—but sharing a common commitment to inclusive and just schools. This conception of leadership requires acknowledgment of the broader leaders that have influenced my work and contributions to this book. There are many people to acknowledge who influenced me and thus provided leadership in my work on this book.

To my students: I wish to acknowledge many of my young students who helped me conceptualize inclusive education. Cha Lee reinforced my belief that it is the teaching of the individual child that is more important than labels. Izzy, Billy, Briel, and Chou Neng taught me that good inclusive classrooms and collaborative teaching are better for meeting everyone's needs. Mane and Phouc showed me that even the most challenging of students with the most significant behavioral, physical, and medical needs should/can/must be permanent members of general education classrooms and that we all benefit from that work. And Dana and Neil let me see the power of classroom community and co-planned instruction on academic growth and self-esteem.

To my teaching partners: Lynn Tucker gave me my first taste of real collaboration and co-teaching, which allowed me to see the power of two teachers in one room. Chris Shelton—the best collaborator one could imagine—taught me first hand just how beautiful co-planning and co-teaching can be.

To my principal and administrative colleagues: Sarah Jerome led by example in teaching the power of community and knowing each and every student in your school. Anna Erbes taught me that where students are educated (the physical location) says a lot about the way a school values them. Deb Hoffman was/is a great mentor and remains, in my opinion, the best principal in the country—her adherence time and time again to the principles of inclusion while "flipping off" those less committed and those who show their incompetence is why her schools always embrace all students and are shining examples for us all. Jack Jorgenson gave me insight into the power of tenacious and visionary inclusive leadership and what it can accomplish for a school district. And, thank you to the many, many principals and school leaders who have worked with us, listened to us, taught us, and informed our work in inclusive leadership.

To my teachers: Several mentors have shaped my thinking about inclusive education. Colleen Capper has been the best scholarly mentor in inclusive schooling I could imagine. Elise Frattura has pushed me to think and act in more meaningful ways. Julie Causton continues to teach me about the whys and hows of inclusion and the power of an inspiring story.

To my colleagues: I am fortunate to have a rich community of inspiring friends and colleagues. Thank you to Richard Shin, Gretchen Lopez, John Rogers, Sonya Douglass Horsford, Cathrine Lugg, Floyd Beachum, Joanne Marshall, Jeff Brooks, Leslie Hazel Bussey, Madeline Hafner, Latish Reed, Charles Payne, Timothy Eatman, Doug Biklen, Sharon Dotger, Marcelle Haddix, Kathy Hinchman, Christy Ashby, Beth Ferri, Tom Bull, Kelly Chandler-Olcott, Paula Kluth, Martin Scanlan, Michael Dantley, Meghan Cosier, Linda Skrla, Tara Affolter, Steve Hoffman, and Kathleen Brown.

To Paul H. Brookes Publishing Co.: A deep debt of gratitude goes to all of the Brookes staff for their commitment to seeing this work come to fruition and making it both better and more accessible.

To my family: Thank you, thank you, thank you to Nancy, Athan, Jeanne, Liz, and Chris for your ongoing commitment and continual drive to make our world more socially just. Your example and tenacity, in your own ways, is inspiring and reassuring. To Ella and Sam, thank you for providing the best daily adventures, for filling my life with magic and excitement, and for giving me a very personal reason to help all school leaders work toward equitable and inclusive schools.

To Ella and Sam, who bring us joy beyond measure, push us to be
stronger and kinder people, and inspire us to do better for *all*

1

The Principal's Role in Inclusive Schools

INCLUSIVE EDUCATION
BECOMES A MOOT POINT

"Systemic change toward inclusive education requires passionate, visionary leaders who are able to build consensus around the goal of providing quality education for all learners. . . . [Study after study found] administrative support and vision to be the most powerful predictor of success of moving toward full inclusion."

—Villa, Thousand, Meyers, and Nevin (1996)

In their statement quoted in the chapter epigraph, Villa, Thousand, Meyers, and Nevin (1996) challenge us to realize that, more than anything else, the role of the school leader is paramount in order to create and maintain inclusive schools. Many factors contribute to the success of inclusive schools and to the benefits that students with and without disabilities, staff, teachers, parents, and communities realize. However, it is the principal who will ultimately make or break a school's ability to be inclusive and to transcend from the rhetoric of inclusion to the reality of embracing the full range of students with and without disabilities as members of the general education learning and social community.

We realize that many educators and principals believe that their schools already "do inclusion." However, almost half of the students with disabilities in the United States are not fully or even partially included in general education or truly connected with their peers (Data Accountability Center, 2010). Many of these students who are not meaningfully or fully included attend the same schools and districts that describe themselves as inclusive. We know that there are wonderful classrooms and schools across the United States that meaningfully and fully include students across the range of disabilities. Nevertheless, we want to be clear, at the onset of this book, that we do not see inclusion as a program to be offered to some students in some classrooms. We see inclusion as an underlying philosophy or way of seeing the world. Inclusion is a way of leading schools that embraces each and every student (those without disabilities, those with mild disabilities, those with autism, those with behavioral challenges, those with significant disabilities, and so on) as full members of the general education academic and social community. We know that it is the principal who needs to make this happen.

THE SHIFTING ROLE OF PRINCIPALS

The position of school principal was introduced about 150 years ago in the United States and other nations. Today's principal position comes from the job of "principal teacher," or head teacher, a role created as state-funded schools were growing. The principal teacher's role was to teach, oversee the other teachers, and manage the organization (Kafka, 2009; Rousmaniere, 2009). Today, most principals do not teach classes, and although the role has always been multifaceted, it has grown increasingly complex and demanding. School organizations at the district, state, and federal level have grown, shaping the demands on principals. The role that schools play in communities has expanded, forcing the position of principal to grow in order to manage these new expectations.

The effective schools research of the 1970s and 1980s proposed that strong school leadership was an essential component of effective schools (see Edmonds, 1979). With that came greater emphasis on the role principals play and a shift from being largely managers to becoming instructional leaders. Instructional leadership became a driving aspect of the principalship, and school organizations and universities worked to give principals the skills to play this growing role. The standards and accountability era has pushed the principalship to expand again by placing greater demands on curricular change and alignment as well as testing and tracking student learning.

Numerous researchers argue that principals today face greater and greater challenges. More demands are placed on them along with greater accountability, with ever-shrinking resources (Kinney, 2003; Langer & Boris-Schacter, 2003; Marshall, 2004; Shields, Larocque, & Oberg, 2002; Strachan, 1997). Almost 20 years ago, principals had numerous interactions each day, up to 400, and up to 150 separate events (Manasse, 1985). Imagine what these numbers look like today.

Today, of the approximately 94,000 principals in this country, 80% are white and 55% male, with the number and percentage of women in school leadership growing (Battle, 2009). The role of these leaders is shifting again. Although principals are expected to manage their schools effectively and be instructional leaders, there is a growing call and need for them to be transformative leaders, to be turn-around leaders, and to be focused on issues of equity. This new push further stretches a very demanding role, but does so in a hopeful direction, as there is great potential power a principal can have to positively affect schools and children.

THE POWER OF THE PRINCIPAL

There is certainly a compelling body of research and wisdom about the important role principals play in creating excellent schools and ensuring equitable learning opportunities for all students (see Cosier, Causton-Theoharis, & Theoharis, 2013; Peterson & Hittie, 2009). The principal has an indirect impact on student learning but plays a direct role in setting and improving the conditions that maximize that learning.

The principal has a direct impact on the scheduling of students, the placement of students into classrooms, the way those classes are set up, and the logistics of running the school. Equally important, the principal has direct impact on the human resources of the school—the quality of the teaching, the way in which the adults work or do not work together, and the expectations for the teachers and staff. In addition, the principal sets the tone and the climate of the school, affecting the school culture; how students, staff, and families are treated; and the general feel of the school. So although the principal does not directly control the math a student learns, he or she has tremendous power to improve the school and thus holds significant promise in creating inclusive learning environments.

PRINCIPALS AND INCLUSIVE SCHOOLS

We know the role principals play in creating and maintaining inclusive schools is paramount. A number of researchers have studied principals in action and have learned key ideas and strategies that are common among examples of success in leading inclusive schools. The following section operationalizes the research examining the role principals play in creating inclusive schools for students with disabilities (see Capper & Frattura, 2008; Capper, Frattura, & Keyes, 2000; McLesky & Waldron, 2002; Pazey & Cole, 2013; Riehl, 2000; Theoharis, 2009). Consistently, principals who are successful at leading fully inclusive schools do the following:

- Set a bold, clear vision of full inclusion

- Engage in collaborative planning and implementation with their staff

- Develop and support teams of professionals

- Reduce fragmentation of initiatives

Setting a Bold, Clear Vision of Full Inclusion

Perhaps the most difficult and most important of these key strategies is laying out a clear vision of full inclusion. Our experience with K–12 schools and the research on this topic is clear that principals need to be out in front of their staffs championing this vision. Principals successful at this do not articulate the current status of inclusion as the goal, nor do they talk in platitudes such as "all children can learn." They are specific in their vision and lofty in setting a high goal. They return to this vision to drive planning and to make decisions for the school in years to come.

Principal Meg describes the bold direction for her school:

> We know that inclusive services are best for students with both significant and mild disabilities. We know that teams of professionals working in inclusive classrooms are better positioned to meet the needs of each learner in the classroom—the high flyer and the struggling student. I believe that each student in this school deserves full and unfettered access to general education, peers, and the general education teachers. This is not up for discussion, as we can and will successfully include all students who come to us. We will figure out how to do this together, but we will do this.

Principal Janice provides a powerful example of maintaining a focus on the vision during the transition to a fully inclusive model. After months of planning how to eliminate self-contained and pullout programs and fully include students with the proper supports in general education across her K–8 school, the service delivery plan was being unveiled by the school's leadership team at a spring staff meeting. After the plan was discussed, Principal Janice stood up and said,

> This is where we are going. We are not going back to the segregated ways of our past. It is no longer an option to exclude some students at this school. This team has worked very hard to come up with the best plan for next year. I recognize we all need support to do this. We will support each other in every way we can.

She continued,

I also recognize that some of you have serious reservations about this direction. I ask that you come with us as we work to make this school a model of inclusion, but if you feel this is not a direction you can head, I will help you find a position where you can be successful. No one here will be allowed to sabotage our efforts. I want each of you to make this work, but I can help you transfer to another school or another profession if you cannot be a part of this. We will become a model of inclusion; if you can't be part of that I have a stack of transfer forms right here.

In the years that followed, when decisions were made or when staff were discussing how to meet the needs of students, Principal Janice was often heard asking, "How does that [particular initiative or structure] fit with our commitment to inclusive education?" Her insistence that total inclusion must not get sidelined by other matters and instead drive decision making was evident in all matters. She continues to keep a bold vision at the forefront of her school.

Engaging in Collaborative Planning and Implementation

In all of the schools we have studied and worked with that are focused on creating fully inclusive services, the decision to become more inclusive might not have been collaboratively set by the staff, but figuring out the best way to create inclusive services was accomplished through collaborative implementation. The principal needed to provide a direction, but she or he brought staff together—special education teachers, general education teachers, support staff such as occupational therapists (OTs) and speech-language pathologists (SLPs), and paraprofessionals—to figure out how the people in their school could make that happen. The planning and implementation was democratic.

Principal Olivia created a specialized leadership team to examine her school's special education service delivery. She made this team open to all who wanted to attend. The team created a variety of options for using the school's existing human resources to become fully inclusive and eliminate self-contained and pullout services. Once they had several ideas, the team worked together to make a coherent service delivery plan for the following year. The team, not the principal, then presented it to the staff to gain broader support.

As is the case with all new initiatives, there were some concerns and bumps in the road on the way to rolling out the plan. Initially, concerns were voiced at the beginning of implementation, and a number of staff got nervous and wanted to go back to the way things used to be, but Principal Olivia made sure the school stayed the course. She brought teachers together to problem-solve and address concerns, but she was clear that the school was not going back.

Every January, this service delivery team begins its work planning for the following year. The members look at the needs and grade levels of projected students for the following year and start making a plan. This is done collaboratively each winter to prepare for the following year. Principal Olivia makes sure this process happens each year but does not control it.

Although many specific attributes are unique to Principal Olivia's school, it provides some key salient ideas for all schools. First, the staff worked together to make an implementation plan over several months. Second, the plan was not abandoned at the first or second or third implementation bump. Finally, given lessons learned and changes in students and staff, each year a team of staff begin thoughtfully planning how to implement a fully inclusive philosophy for the following year.

Developing and Supporting Teams

A key strategy that principals must engage in is to develop teams of specialists and generalists to carry out the fully inclusive plan. Developing teams takes on different forms, but their core goal is to bring together professionals who will share responsibility to work together to meet the needs of the wide range of learners in an inclusive setting under their joint care. This requires revising the roles many professionals have played in their schools for years and building trust and understanding between those members. It is essential that, in addition to developing teams, the principal supports those teams and provides them common planning time.

In an effort to develop teams at her high school, Principal Natalie assigned special education teachers to be content area special education teachers. This change meant her school no longer ran classes of specific content areas that were only for students in special education and no longer maintained self-contained special education programs. Now, all special education staff members were used to support students (i.e., co-plan and co-deliver instruction) in general education. Principal Natalie ensured special education teachers had common planning time with the content teachers they were directly working with and she treated those special education teachers as part of the content team. She provided time for each special education teacher over the summer to meet with, get to know, and become familiar with the content teachers and the school curriculum. Natalie found funds to pay her staff for this time. As time passed, the special education teachers became integral parts of many content area teams, bringing their expertise in differentiation, modification, individualization, and lesson planning.

In creating teams at the elementary level, Principal Tracy paired special education teachers with two or three classroom teachers at his school. Each year Tracy took teacher volunteers who were interested in working together, and this provided the majority of special education and general education teams, but each year he had to make a couple of teams based on who he saw as the best partners for that year. Those teaching teams were given time to meet each week and were expected to use it. In addition, Principal Tracy used professional development monies to provide team-building time before each school year began and provided as much paid time after school as needed (or used half-day substitute teachers) so the teams could work together co-planning and co-creating their instructional program.

Middle school Principal Tim provides support and common planning time as well. Tim works and reworks the master schedule each spring. During this process, he makes sure staffing is such that all students with disabilities are in general education classrooms; the school no longer uses sections of pullout classes or self-contained special education programs. Principal Tim uses all of his general and special education staff to make up teams that will co-plan and co-deliver instruction. He does not have the human resources to have one special education teacher in each room or to allow his special education teachers to collaborate with one or two general education teachers, but he does not allow this to be a barrier to a fully inclusive service model—he spreads his special education support across enough rooms that students with disabilities are not overloaded into one section. He balances that with a reasonable number of general education teachers for his special education staff to plan with. He gathers feedback from his staff to drive this process. He carefully works the schedule and staffing plan, creating common planning time for grade-level teams and, perhaps more important, for smaller instructional teams of special and general educators.

In addition, we have seen a number of principals, including some of those mentioned previously, who brought in outside expertise to help teams develop. Tracy wrote a grant to provide a one-third time collaboration facilitator who met with teams, helping them learn to work together, use planning time efficiently, and become a more effective team. Other principals have offered team development workshops over the summer, led by collaboration experts to help develop teams for the following year. Still other principals have offered ongoing collaboration courses for professional development credit. Some of the leaders have worked with local universities to tap into collaboration courses that were being offered, allowing teachers to audit classes, for example. Others worked with district or regional professional developers to offer similar professional development. Each principal who leads an inclusive school has realized that adults need to work together in profoundly new ways and that most teachers and staff are not well equipped to do this. Thus, the principals' work in developing teams and providing support plays a key role in the success of inclusive schools. Collaborative teams are also discussed in Chapter 5 and touched on in Chapter 4.

Reducing Fragmentation of Initiatives

Previously, we stated that inclusion is not a program but a guiding philosophy for making decisions about where and how we educate students. Thus, when schools move toward fully including all students, this decision cannot be separate from other changes and programs of the school. Principal leadership is important in two ways in reducing fragmentation of initiatives. First, we found that successful principals acted as gatekeepers, knowing that they could not ask their teachers to do too many new things at once. As they were moving toward fully inclusive services, they reduced the other new initiatives or programs that were rolled out in their school. This meant that the principals themselves did not initiate many other changes during the early years of fully inclusive services. They also pushed back against district pressures to take on more than a couple of new changes. In this capacity of reducing fragmentation, principals made sure, as new staff joined the school, that they understood the philosophy and the inclusive expectations.

Second, successful principals made sure that their commitments to inclusion were a part of everything at their school, from new curriculum and instructional approaches to extracurricular activities and programs. For example, at Principal Steve's high school, when it adopted a new math series, Steve made sure the special education teachers who were co-planning and co-delivering instruction in math went to training and orientation about the new math series with the other math teachers. He made sure they all had teacher's manuals and had enough materials (e.g., manipulatives, calculators) to be used in large- and small-group inclusive instruction.

Principal Ann's middle school was taking on 6+1 traits of writing approach as part of the school's literacy program. Ann made sure the special education teachers were part of that professional development. More important, as the teams planned their writing instruction, Principal Ann made sure that the needs of all students were considered (from mild to significant) as lessons were planned and executed. As a result, the teachers never imagined that Jerry (a student labeled with an intellectual disability) and Ali (a student labeled with autism) could write so much and grow so much.

In addition to ensuring that inclusion became a part of improving the teaching and learning, successful principals made sure inclusion was also a part of extracurricular activities. At Principal Meg's elementary school, the district brought in a local nonprofit to run after-school programming. Meg would not accept the nonprofit organization's hesitance to serve students with significant disabilities. She worked with them to ensure that students with disabilities had access. She also provided guidance and insistence that students with disabilities were authentic members of the after-school program and were treated as such, and that they were not separated from their peers.

The actions and initiative exhibited by these principals provide examples of how reducing fragmentation allowed the inclusive philosophy to blossom in their schools. When this is implemented, inclusion is not seen as a program that will come and go or a service for only some students—inclusion becomes "the way we do things around here."

COMMONLY ASKED QUESTIONS ABOUT INCLUSION

Q. When reducing fragmentation of initiatives, does that mean that I let some initiatives go while focusing on inclusion?

A. Some initiatives make sense to just integrate with inclusion. Some make sense to wait while the staff gain the skills and capacity to serve all learners inclusively. It makes sense to take a close look at what your staff are being asked to learn and try to prioritize these new initiatives or merge them together.

Q. When developing a team to work on issues of inclusion, who should be involved?

A. Many principals make the decision to include representation from all grade levels and special education. Others use the existing leadership team. Still others have left the door open to anyone who wants to work on these issues. There are pros and cons to each decision.

Q. I'm afraid not all of my staff will buy into more inclusion. What can I do about that?

A. We have never seen a school in which there has not been at least some resistance to inclusion. So, you need to recognize that resistance is a normal part of this work. You also cannot be stopped by a vocal minority.

Q. What are the barriers to full inclusion?

A. The barriers can take a variety of forms that include teachers holding tightly onto old roles and ways of providing services, ineffective teams, lack of common planning for teams, structural/logistical issues, and lack of vision and inclusion.

Q. Is it better to write the vision myself and then share it with the staff or to have the staff write the vision with me?

A. In our experience, we have seen it done both ways. Either way will work, but one thing is certain: when you get the vision you want, clearly state to all that this is the direction the staff are moving in and take a clear leadership role in carrying it out. Also, don't waste a lot of time creating a vision with the staff. The team can lose momentum before even getting started. It is often best to start with your vision and allow the staff to discuss.

CONCLUSION

Leading toward a fully inclusive school requires a lot of the principal. We recognize that this is challenging. Despite increasing pressures and changing roles, principal leadership is essential so that each and every student has full access to the general education curriculum, instruction, and peers. This leadership sets the conditions for each student to reach her or his full academic and social potential. We know that schools cannot become inclusive or maintain full inclusion without the careful planning, support, and leadership of good principals.

NOTES

2

Special Education

WHAT DO YOU CHOOSE TO SEE?
WEEDS OR WILDFLOWERS?

"Before I was a principal, I taught seventh- and eighth-grade English. Sure I had students with disabilities in my classes, but I certainly didn't have a background in special education."

—Kris (principal)

We begin with the question that many have asked when they began work in this field: What is special education? In this chapter, we answer that question, along with these others: Who receives special education? What does *disability* mean? Why should people be cautious of labels? What does all this terminology mean? What are the different categories of disabilities? At the end of this chapter, we also answer other commonly asked questions.

This chapter identifies the important concepts and ideas that are essential to understand for anyone in the field of special education. By knowing this information, principals can understand the larger special education system as they lead an inclusive school.

WHAT IS SPECIAL EDUCATION?

Simply put, *special education* is individualized instruction designed to meet the unique needs of certain students. This type of customized instruction may require a student to have accommodations or modifications to his or her classwork. *Accommodations* are adaptations to the curriculum that do not fundamentally alter or lower standards (e.g., test location, student response method). *Modifications* are changes to the curriculum that do alter the expectations. Examples of modifications include changes to the course content, timing, or test presentation. Any student who receives special education services may receive specialized materials (e.g., books on tape), services (e.g., speech and language services), equipment (e.g., a communication system), or different teaching strategies (e.g., visual notes) (Individuals with Disabilities Education Improvement Act [IDEA] of 2004, PL 108-446). For example, a student who is deaf may require the services of a sign language interpreter in order to follow along in the classroom. A student who has autism may require specialized materials such as a visual schedule to prepare for the changing routines in the day. A student with a learning disability may require additional reading instruction or extended time for completing written assignments.

Special education is a part of general education. It is a system of supports to help students learn the general education curriculum. The legal definition under IDEA 2004 of *special education* is "specially designed instruction, at no cost to the child's parents, to meet the needs of a student with a disability" (PL 108-446; § 1401 [25]).

This definition recognizes that some children have difficulty learning, behaving, or physically engaging in general education and, because of such disabilities, need individualized supports to help them to build their skills and abilities to reach their full potential in school. These additional services do not cost the students' parents any money and are funded by the local and federal governments. These IDEA-defined and mandated services are considered entitlements.

SPECIAL EDUCATION IS A SERVICE, NOT A PLACE

In the past, when the term *special education* was used, a special place came to mind. People thought of a room, a school, or another separate place to which children with disabilities went to receive different and special education. This notion, however, is rapidly changing. Special education is no longer limited to a specific location. It has been established that all children—even children with autism, severe disabilities, and emotional or behavioral disabilities—learn best in classroom settings with their general education peers (Causton-Theoharis & Theoharis, 2008; Peterson & Hittie, 2009). Special education services are portable services (e.g., help with reading, math, speech skills) that can be brought directly to individual children. Special education occurs in general education classrooms all over the United States and the rest of the world. This aligns with the stated legal purpose of special education. Under IDEA 2004, *special education* means "specially designed instruction . . . to meet the unique needs of a child with a disability" (§300.39). This "specially designed instruction" means "adapting, as appropriate to the needs of an eligible child . . . the content, methodology, or delivery of instruction" in order 1) "to address the unique needs of the child that result from the child's disability" and 2) "to ensure access of the child to the general curriculum, so that the child can meet the educational standards within the jurisdiction of the public agency that apply to all children" (IDEA 2004, PL 108-446; §300.39[b][3]). It is clear under IDEA that special education is supposed to ensure access to the general curriculum. It is important for principals to remember this purpose.

The primary means for ensuring this access is for students with disabilities to be educated primarily in general education settings; this is called *inclusive education*. In inclusive classrooms, teachers and principals should ensure that children with special needs are part of the general education curriculum, instruction, and social scene as much as possible within the least restrictive environment (LRE). Chapter 3 explores inclusive education and will describe more fully the concept of LRE.

WHO RECEIVES SPECIAL EDUCATION?

Every year, under IDEA 2004, more than 6 million students in the United States between the ages of 3 and 21 receive special education services (National Center for Education Statistics [NCES], 2011). In other words, roughly 11% of all school-age children qualify for special education services because they have disabilities.

Under IDEA 2004, the definition of a student with a disability is "one who has certain disabilities and who, because of the impairment, needs special education and related services" (PL 108-446; § 1401 [3]). Each student qualifies for special education because he or she has at least one type of disability. Each of the different types of disabilities is defined and described later in this chapter.

When one examines the population of students who receive special education, several disturbing trends appear in the areas of gender, socioeconomic status, and race.

First, even though the numbers of males and females in the general school population are equal, the population receiving special education is roughly two-thirds male (U.S. Department of Education, 2007). Second, the poverty rate is proportionately much higher among students who qualify for special education than in the entire school population (U.S. Department of Education, 2007). Last, a disproportionate number of certain racial or ethnic groups are served in special education. For example, because African Americans make up 14% of the general population, one might assume that only 14% of students who qualify for special education would be African American (Turnbull, Turnbull, Shank, & Smith, 2004). In fact, African American students represent 44.9% of the total number of students labeled as having learning disabilities (U.S. Department of Education, 2007). Further, African American students are three times more likely than Caucasian students to receive special education and related services.

WHAT DOES *DISABILITY* MEAN?

Disability categories are used to "classify and think about the problems developing children may encounter" (Contract Consultants, IAC, 1997, p. 8, as cited in Kluth, 2003). Understanding a student's label is only the beginning point in learning about a child. A child's disability label reveals nothing about the student's individual gifts, talents, and strengths. A disability is one of many parts of a student. A disability does not describe who a person is; it describes only one aspect of the person.

To illustrate this point, take a moment to write down five descriptors about yourself. What did you include? Your list might include *mother, father, teacher, principal, lover of nature, daughter,* or *outgoing.* Did your list include deficiencies? Probably not. Most of us do not think of ourselves through the lens of deficit. The same is true for any individual with a disability. That person's area of disability is one (possibly very small) part of who he or she is.

SOCIAL CONSTRUCTION OF DISABILITY

It is also important to recognize that people create disability categories and that those categories shift and change over time. Medical professionals, teachers, and researchers, along with the federal government, have created these categories. These are not static categories; they do and have changed. An extreme example of how disability is constructed is that, at one point in time, to qualify as having a cognitive disability (or mental retardation, as used in federal legislation), a person needed to have an IQ of 80 or below. In 1973, the federal government lowered the cutoff IQ score to 70 points or below. So, in essence, with the single stroke of a pen, hundreds of thousands of people were "cured" of mental retardation (Ashby, 2008; Blatt, 1987).

Once created, these categories are reinforced. In other words, people see mainly what they are looking for. Once a student is assigned a label, educators begin seeing the child through a different lens—the lens of disability. As we were observing a student for a research project in a third-grade classroom, we observed this very notion. All of the students were busy working and talking as they finished their art projects. The room was bustling and busy. Suddenly, the art teacher shouted, "Jamie, that is the last time." The teacher walked to the chalkboard and wrote Jamie's name down. Nearly all of the students were talking, yet Jamie, who happens to have a label of emotional disturbance, was noticed for being too talkative or out of line. From where we were sitting, Jamie's behavior looked no different from that of many of the other students.

Disability categories are created, and then people determine who qualifies and who does not. Have you ever worked with someone who had a label even though you really did not think he or she had a disability? Have you ever seen a student who did not qualify for special education even though you thought he or she might? Disability labels are not hard and fast rules that describe people; they are indicators of patterns of difficulty for individuals and are determined by the perceptions of other people.

LABELS: PROCEED WITH CAUTION

On the one hand, many believe labels to be helpful for defining a common language for parents and professionals. This common language allows students access to certain supports and services that they need. In a way, a label is the necessary first step toward certain services.

On the other hand, there are real problems with the labeling or categorizing of individuals. Kliewer and Biklen stated that labeling students can be a "demeaning process frequently contributing to stigmatization and leading to social and educational isolation" (1996, p. 83). The use of and overreliance on disability labels poses many problems. Disability labels can lead to stereotyping by causing teachers to see certain students in one, and only one, way. Labeling tends to highlight the differences among people. For example, when a student is assigned a label, teachers and principals begin to notice the differences between that student and his or her peers. Labels can lead to poor self-esteem as students begin to see themselves differently because of such labels. Last, labels convey the impression of permanence, even though, in some cases, students are only "disabled" when they are in school. Unfortunately, labels give professionals a real sense of security. They allow professionals to believe that "disability categories are static, meaningful, and well understood when in fact they are none of these things" (Kluth, 2005, p. 7).

Throughout this book, we use the language that is most common to the current educational system. We are well aware, however, of the real problems and, at times, dangers of thinking about difference in these ways. Some people use the term *dis/ability* (with a slash) to indicate that all students should focus on their individual abilities. Although we prefer the word *dis/ability*, we purposefully use the language most common to education so that readers can easily connect this information to other information from the field.

THE ALPHABET SOUP OF EDUCATIONAL TERMINOLOGY

Alphabet soup: that is how we sometimes describe the use of acronyms in the field of special education. Understanding the language of special education can take a long time. The following is an alphabetical listing of several educational terms that are often used as acronyms:

ADD/ADHD: attention deficit disorder and/or attention-deficit/hyperactivity disorder

BIP: behavior intervention plan

CBI: community-based instruction

DS: Down syndrome

EBD: emotional behavioral disturbance

ED: emotional disturbance

ESY: extended school year

FAPE: free appropriate public education

FBA: functional behavioral assessment

HI: hearing impaired

ID: intellectual disability

IDEA: Individuals with Disabilities Education Act

IEP: individualized education program

LRE: least restrictive environment

MR: mental retardation

OI: orthopedic impairment

OT: occupational therapist

PBS: positive behavior support

PT: physical therapist

SL: speech and language

SLD: specific learning disability

SLP: speech-language pathologist

TBI: traumatic brain injury

VI: visual impairment

FEDERALLY RECOGNIZED CATEGORIES OF DISABILITY

How many different categories of disability are you aware of? There are 13 federal categories of disability. Every student who receives special education services has received a formal label representing one of the 13 categories. Now, without looking ahead in this book, take a moment to jot down on a separate piece of paper as many of the 13 disability categories as you can. Compare your list with the information provided in the next paragraph.

The 13 categories of disability include the following: 1) autism, 2) deafblindness, 3) deafness, 4) ED, 5) hearing impairment, 6) ID, 7) multiple disabilities, 8) OI, 9) other health impairments, 10) specific learning disabilities, 11) speech and language impairments, 12) TBI, and 13) VI including blindness. The sections below include the IDEA 2004 definition for each; however, the most useful way to understand each disability is to listen carefully to the people who have been labeled with the disability and understand the disability deeply. Therefore, after each of the definitions, we include voices of people who have been labeled with each of the particular disabilities. These voices are not meant to be representative examples; one person cannot possibly represent the entire population of students who have the same disability. Note the differences between the legal definitions and the definitions that the people themselves use. It is interesting that the legal definitions focus on what students cannot do or the difficulties that they have, whereas the student voices focus more on the gifts and abilities of each individual.

Autism

Autism is defined by law as a developmental disability that significantly affects verbal and nonverbal communication and social interaction and adversely affects educational performance; autism is generally evident before age 3. Characteristics often associated with autism are engaging in repetitive activities and stereotyped movements, resistance to change in daily routines or the environment, and unusual responses to sensory experiences (34 C.F.R. § 300.8 [c][1][i]).

A person who has autism and lives with it every day offers a quite different definition of the disability:

> Some aspects of autism may be good or bad depending only on how they are perceived. For example, hyperfocusing is a problem if you're hyperfocusing on your feet and miss the traffic light change. On the other hand, hyperfocusing is a great skill for working on intensive projects. This trait is particularly well suited to freelancers and computer work. I would never argue that autism is all good or merely a difference. I do find that my autism is disabling. However, that doesn't mean that it is all bad or that I mean I want to be someone else. (Molton, 2000, p. 46)

Another individual with autism described it this way: "I believe Autism is a marvelous occurrence of nature, not a tragic example of the human mind gone wrong.

In many cases, Autism can also be a kind of genius undiscovered" (O'Neill, 1999, p. 14, as cited in Kluth, 2005, p. 3).

Deafblindness

Deafblindness is defined by law as concomitant (simultaneous) hearing and visual impairments, the combination of which causes such severe communication and other developmental and educational needs that they cannot be accommodated in special education programs solely for children with deafness or children with blindness (34 C.F.R. § 300.8 [c][2]). In other words, students with deafblindness have both hearing and visual impairments. The population of students with deafblindness constitutes only 0.0001% of the special education population. Therefore, most readers probably will not support someone with this disability label. Many people who are deaf and blind learn to use tactile sign, a form of sign language that is felt with the hands.

Helen Keller is one of the most famous examples of a person with deafblindness. She wrote very articulately about what it was like to live with this label in her autobiography entitled *The Story of My Life* (1903). One quote from Keller described how she interacted with the world: "The best and most beautiful things in the world cannot be seen or even touched. They must be felt within the heart" (p. 6).

Deafness

Deafness is legally defined as a hearing impairment so severe that a child's educational performance is adversely affected; people with deafness have difficulty, with or without amplification, in processing linguistic information (34 C.F.R. § 300.8 [c][3]). Students who qualify for special education under the category of deafness typically use sign language. These individuals can gain access to the general education curriculum through the use of a sign language interpreter, through oral methods of speech reading, or by reading other people's lips and facial expressions.

A deaf college student identified as Mavis shared her experiences living as a deaf person:

> It is true. Every weekend, I ride my high quality road racing bicycle at high speeds (sometimes as fast as 40 mph on the flats) with a bunch of men from my bicycle club. I am the only deaf person in that 500 member club. I also enjoy going to the shooting range to fire handguns and socialize. (Mavis, 2003)

Emotional Disturbance

ED is legally defined as

> A condition exhibiting one or more of the following characteristics for a long period of time and to a marked degree that adversely affects a child's educational performance:
>
> a. An inability to learn that cannot be explained by intellectual, sensory, or health factors.
> b. An inability to build or maintain satisfactory interpersonal relationships with peers and teachers.

c. Inappropriate types of behavior or feelings under normal circumstances.
d. A general pervasive mood of unhappiness or depression.
e. A tendency to develop physical symptoms or fears associated with personal or school problems. (34 C.F.R. § 300.8 [c][4][i])

These students make up about 8% of the special education population. This category of disability relates to how students behave. For a student to qualify for this category of disability, the student's behavior should look significantly different from that of peers (Taylor, Smiley, & Richards, 2009).

Kerri, who has ED, describes it this way:

> I misinterpret half of what [people] say to me and translate it to mean they don't want to be my friend anymore. Why should they? I am not worth their time or love or attention. Then I get angry with them and I turn on them. Hurt them before they can hurt me. It is so stupid, and I realize it later, but only after it is too late. (Information on bipolar and other mental health disorders, n.d.)

Hearing Impairment

Being identified as having a *hearing impairment* means that there is an impairment in hearing, whether permanent or fluctuating, that adversely affects a child's educational performance but that is not included under the definition of *deafness* (34 C.F.R. § 300.8 [c][5]). Students who have hearing impairments generally do not use sign language, because the hearing that they do have is useful to them. Instead, they might use an amplification system and receive training in lipreading.

One individual (Sarahjane Thompson) with hearing impairment described her experience:

> The way I tend to explain [hearing impairment] is that it's not necessarily that you can't hear the words that people are using, it's that you hear sounds that resemble words, but you can't quite figure out what the sounds are. Like when a hearing person only just hears something, and asks someone to repeat themselves. Like that. Except for me it's way more frequent. So that's why I tend to use other strategies to figure out what's going on. I lip-read. . . . But lip-reading isn't perfect. A lot of the words look the same and so it's hard for me to use it exclusively to talk to someone. I tend to guess a lot. I'll catch most of a sentence and then sort of try to fill in the gaps myself. Usually it works. Sometimes it doesn't. . . . Every now and then I'll mis-hear an entire sentence and my brain will fill in the random words that sort of fit the syllables and sounds, but together those words do not make sense at all. . . . It's just so normal for me to be hearing impaired. People ask me what it's like to be [hearing impaired] and I just don't have a perfect answer for them. "What's it like to be able to hear?" There's no real comparison and so I don't really know what is different about it. Obviously hearing people can hear more and understand more sounds, but what does that mean? It can be really hard to explain. It's all about perception. (Williams & Thompson, 2008)

Intellectual Disability

The MR label is legally assigned to students who have significantly subaverage general intellectual functioning, existing concurrently with impairments in adaptive behavior and manifested during the developmental period, that adversely affects a child's educational performance (34 C.F.R. § 300.8 [c][6]). The term *mental retardation* is cited in IDEA 2004 but was changed in 2010 under Rosa's Law (PL 111-256) to *intellectual disability*.

The definition, however, did not change. Another term commonly used is *cognitive disability*. This category constitutes 8.86% of the special education population. People with ID vary greatly. Some students have speech and can write, whereas other students do not use speech and are unable to write. Lacking the ability to write or speak, however, does not mean that the person has no ideas or no desire to communicate with others. These students tend to deeply desire connections with others and, when given the tools to communicate, engage with other students and with the content.

The following is a first-person account from someone labeled with cognitive disabilities:

> What I would like is for you to understand that my biggest problem is not a neurological dysfunction. It is being misunderstood by people who think my problems are due to poor parenting. My mom has really tried to teach me proper social behaviors, but it just does not click all the time. Sometimes I can't remember the social rules. (FAS Community Resource Center, 2008)

Ollie Webb explained his life with ID:

> I was often the target of cruel jokes. It was easy to take advantage of me. People called me retarded . . . [but] I worked out there—17 years—and I made salads, sandwiches, and soup, and washed pots and pans. You name it, I done it out there. . . .One time I came in and the boss said, "I am going to take you off of salads." I said, "Why?" He said, "Cause you can't read." I said, "It make no difference. I can make salads and sandwiches." I said, "It make no damn difference.". . . . It came time to leave the sad word retarded [to history]. . . . To say that people should be known by their names [and accomplishments], not by their disabilities, I ain't different from you. I am the same as you. I got a name, and I want you to call me by my name. My name is Ollie Wayne Webb. (Schalock & Braddock, 2002, pp. 55–57)

Multiple Disabilities

The term *multiple disabilities* is legally defined as concomitant impairments (e.g., ID–blindness, ID–OI), the combination of which causes such severe educational needs that the student cannot be accommodated in a special educational setting solely for one of the impairments. The term does not include deafblindness (34 C.F.R. § 300.8 [c][7]). Roughly 2% of the special education population is considered to have multiple disabilities.

Orthopedic Impairments

The term *orthopedic impairment* refers to a severe OI that adversely affects a child's educational performance. The term includes impairments caused by congenital impairments (e.g., clubfoot, absence of a body part), impairments caused by disease (e.g., poliomyelitis, bone tuberculosis), and impairments from other causes (e.g., cerebral palsy, amputations, fractures or burns that cause contractures) (34 C.F.R. § 300.8 [c][8]).

Angela Gabel, a high school student with cerebral palsy who uses a wheelchair, described herself and her experience in school as follows:

> When you see me, I think the first thing you would notice is that I'm a pretty positive person. I love to listen to music, go horseback riding, and draw. . . . When I was in elementary school . . .

I had friends and liked to play the same games as everyone else, but the teachers were always worried that I was too fragile and would hurt myself. (Gabel, 2006, p. 35)

Other Health Impairments

Other health impairment is legally defined as having limited strength, vitality, or alertness to environmental stimuli, resulting in limited alertness with respect to the educational environment, that

    a. is due to chronic or acute health problems such as asthma, attention deficit disorder or attention deficit hyperactivity disorder, diabetes, epilepsy, a heart condition, hemophilia, lead poisoning, leukemia, nephritis, rheumatic fever, and sickle cell anemia; and

    b. adversely affects a child's educational performance. (34 C.F.R. § 300.8 [c][9])

This impairment includes students who have ADHD. The label *ADHD* is assigned to students who have difficulty maintaining attention, knowing when to slow down, or organizing themselves to finish tasks (American Psychiatric Association, 2000). Obviously, not everyone who has each of these disorders qualifies for special education, but if such a condition has been diagnosed by a medical professional and adversely affects a student's educational performance (and if the student needs additional supports), he or she is likely to qualify.

Brian explained his life with attention disorders:

As you can tell by my writing style i run all over the place. give mwe [sic] a task and directions it's done asap. give me time to think about it, it's done in my head but i can't complete the task. (Living with ADD, 2004)

Specific Learning Disabilities

An SLD is legally defined as a disorder in one or more of the basic psychological processes involved in understanding or using spoken or written language; it may manifest itself in an imperfect ability to listen, think, speak, read, write, spell, or do mathematical calculations. The term includes such conditions as perceptual disabilities, brain injury, minimal brain dysfunction, dyslexia, and developmental aphasia. The term does not include learning problems that are primarily the results of visual, hearing, or motor disabilities; of ID; of ED; or of environmental, cultural, or economic disadvantages (34 C.F.R. § 300.8 [c][10]).

Almost half of all students categorized as having disabilities fall under this category. This is the most frequently occurring disability; thus, you are quite likely to work with students who have the label of specific learning disability.

In an article about being a student with a learning disability, Caitlin Norah Callahan wrote about her advice to others:

I believe one key idea is to find one's own definition of the dual identity within oneself as a learner and as a student. The learner is the one who makes an effort to be curious, involved and motivated. Not all knowledge is taught in school. It is the student identity that gets labeled as the disabled. The "learning disability" should not be allowed to overwhelm one's desire to attain knowledge. The learner in you must prevent it. (Callahan, 1997)

Speech and Language Impairments

Speech or language impairment is legally defined as a communication disorder such as stuttering, impaired articulation, a language impairment, or a voice impairment that adversely affects a child's educational performance (34 C.F.R. § 300.8 [c][11]).

This is the second most common disability category. Approximately 20% of students who qualify for special education are served under this category. Students who qualify for this disability have a wide range of impairment. Some students who receive speech and language services have difficulty with articulation or fluency (e.g., stuttering). Other students might not use speech.

What follows is a story from a person who did not have speech in his early years but who later was able to communicate through the use of a communication system. This story illustrates the frustration inherent in not having a reliable method of speech:

> I know what it is like to be fed potatoes all my life. After all potatoes are a good basic food for everyday, easy to fix in many different ways. I hate potatoes! But then who knew that but me? I know what it is like to be dressed in reds and blues when my favorite colors are mint greens, lemon yellows, and pinks. I mean really can you imagine [what it is like not to communicate]? Mama found me one night curled up in a ball in my bed crying, doubled over in pain. I couldn't explain to her where or how I hurt. So, after checking me over the best she could, she thought I had a bad stomachache due to constipation. Naturally, a quick cure for that was an enema. It did not help my earache at all! (Paul-Brown & Diggs, 1993, p. 8).

Traumatic Brain Injury

TBI is legally defined as an acquired injury to the brain caused by an external physical force, resulting in total or partial functional disability or psychosocial impairment, or both, that adversely affects a child's educational performance. The term applies to open or closed head injuries resulting in impairments in one or more areas, such as cognition; language; memory; attention; reasoning; abstract thinking; judgment; problem solving; sensory, perceptual, and motor abilities; psychosocial behavior; physical functions; information processing; and speech. The term does not include brain injuries that are congenital, degenerative, or induced by birth trauma (34 C.F.R. § 300.8 [c][12]).

This type of disability differs from the others because it is acquired during the person's lifetime (e.g., car accident, blow to the head). People are not born with this condition—instead, they acquire the disability. The emotional adjustment to acquiring a disability is an issue not only for the student but also for parents or guardians and teachers.

A teenager who endured a TBI reflected on what she saw as her new life:

> The three-month coma that followed and the years of rehabilitation are only a blur to me. I slowly awoke over the next two years becoming aware of my surroundings as well as myself and my inabilities, one being that I could no longer sing as I was left with a severe speech impediment. (Parker, 2008)

Visual Impairment, Including Blindness

A VI is legally defined as an impairment in vision that, even with correction, adversely affects a child's educational performance. The term includes both partial sight and blindness (34 C.F.R. § 300.8 [c][13]).

The services received by students under this category of disability differ depending on the severity or type of VI. Some students with VIs use magnifiers and larger-print texts; students who have no vision receive mobility training (or training on how to walk around their environment) and instruction in how to read braille.

Distribution of Students with Disabilities in Each Category

How many students qualify for each of the different types of disabilities? The pie graph shown in Figure 2.1 depicts the percentages of students receiving special education services from ages 6 to 21 who fall under each of the categories of disabilities. As Figure 2.1 indicates, the high-incidence (or most common) disabilities are learning disabilities, speech and language disabilities, ID, and other health impairments. The rest of the categories are considered low incidence (or not as common).

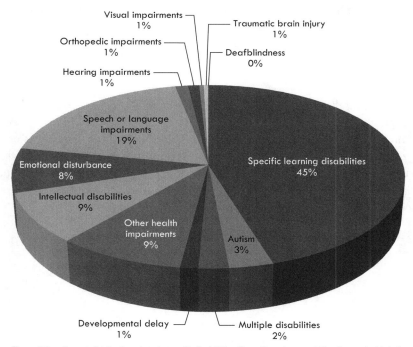

Figure 2.1. Percent distribution of students with disabilities. (From Data Accountability Center. [n.d.]. *Individuals with Disabilities Education Act [IDEA] data.* Retrieved 1 December, 2008 from http://www.ideadata.org/docs/PartBTrendData/B2A.html)

Now that you have read through each of the definitions of disabilities, we reiterate the importance of knowing these definitions, but keep in mind that this is only a (very small) step in understanding a student. Chapter 4 focuses more on how to think about students in general, with very little focus on individual disabilities.

COMMONLY ASKED QUESTIONS ABOUT SPECIAL EDUCATION

Q. I do not have a background in special education. How much do I need to know?

A. As the instructional leader of a school, you need to be well versed in the language and the law of special education. You not only will be providing guidance to teachers about how to best support students, but you sit on the committee on special education (CSE) and IEP teams as a leader in the process. The more you know about the categories of disabilities, how students get labels, and the myriad of support possibilities, the better off you will be.

Q. Where can I turn for more support in the area of special education?

A. Your district special education director is a good place to start. Also, look to your local colleges and universities for knowledge and expertise in the area of special education. Finally, your special education teachers are likely quite knowledgeable about special education.

CONCLUSION

Understanding disability is critical to understanding the larger systems of special education. Nonetheless, the only way to truly understand certain individual students is to get to know people who live with those disabilities. Reading the definitions of the 13 federal categories of disability is just the first step to understanding the students you support. Having covered some of the basics of special education, we commence the joyful work of helping the reader to learn about individual students and support them in the classroom. Chapter 3 focuses on including students with disabilities.

NOTES

_____

_____

_____

_____

_____

_____

_____

_____

_____

_____

_____

_____

_____

_____

_____

_____

_____

_____

_____

_____

_____

_____

_____

_____

_____

_____

_____

3

Inclusive Education

THE EVOLUTION OF SWIMMING LESSONS:
SURPRISINGLY SIMILAR TO THE EVOLUTION
OF INCLUDING STUDENTS WITH
DISABILITIES IN GENERAL EDUCATION.

"When I think back to my own schooling experience, students with disabilities did not go to school with me. They were bussed to a school in the neighboring district. Although inclusion isn't new, it is new to our generation of educator, because we did not live it ourselves as kids. Our students now get to see the world differently, and better, because they are growing up in an inclusive school and learning that diversity in all its forms—including ability/disability—is normal and to be embraced."

—Sydney (principal)

We begin this chapter on inclusive education with the reminder from the previous chapter that the purpose of special education outlined in IDEA 2004 (PL 108-446) is to ensure students with disabilities access to general curriculum. This is done most authentically and effectively through inclusive education. In this chapter, we identify the concepts necessary to understanding inclusive education, such as belonging, the history of inclusive education, major legal concepts, the definition of inclusive education, indicators of inclusive education, IEPs, and commonly asked questions.

BELONGING

"To be rooted is perhaps the most important and least recognized need of the human soul."

—Simone Weil (2001)

One central reason that kids are being included in general education settings is that every child, with or without disabilities, has the right to belong. All human beings desire friendships, relationships, and academic challenge. Kids with disabilities are no different.

Think for a moment about yourself. Think of a time you believed that you truly belonged somewhere. Was it a group, a club, a sports team, or a work environment? Now think about your behavior in that setting. How did you behave? How did you feel? If someone looked at you, how did you act? Most people are more willing to take risks, to contribute, to share, and to learn in such environments. When you feel connected to a group of people, you are likely more talkative, more engaged, and more willing to be yourself. The same is true for children.

Now, on the contrary, think of a time you believed you did not belong or were ostracized from a group. How did you behave? How did you feel? In those situations, many people respond by being withdrawn and quiet, shutting themselves off from the group. Or, a person might respond by leaving the situation or getting angry. The same is true for children in school. It is essential to feel connected to a group or part of the school community. Not only is this important for self-worth, but it is also important for learning.

When working with a group of administrators, teachers, and paraprofessionals, we asked the preceding questions. Their responses are shown in Table 3.1.

Examine the responses shown in the table. How do they relate to students in school? Have you seen students in school who feel sick, angry, withdrawn, or hurt? Have you seen students who behave in ways that let you know they do not believe

Table 3.1. Feelings associated with inclusion and exclusion

When I was included	When I was excluded
I felt loved	I was angry
I felt cared for	I was withdrawn
I took risks	I was quiet
I felt smart	I was hurt
I was myself	I cried
I laughed often	I felt sick
I was creative	I did not participate
I was open to learn	I tried to leave the group

that they belong? On the other hand, have you noticed kids who are engaged, acting like themselves, and freely taking risks? In our own roles as teachers and a principal, we have observed kids who regularly felt connected and those who did not. Helping students feel that they belong is one of the most important jobs of the paraprofessional and teacher, under the leadership of the principal.

If a system of special education excludes kids and puts them in rooms, hallways, or schools that are separate from the general education population, the children will not behave as well or learn as well. School administrators and teachers all over the country are rethinking the practice of isolating students with disabilities in one room (Causton-Theoharis & Theoharis, 2008; McLeskey & Waldron, 2006). Isolating students in this way causes them to feel different from everyone else and not part of the larger school community. This type of segregation has real consequences for students' self-esteem and ability to learn (Peterson & Hittie, 2009). Inclusive education was built on the foundation that all people have the basic human right to belong.

THE HISTORY OF INCLUSIVE EDUCATION

You might have attended a school in which students with disabilities were educated down the hall, in a separate wing, or in a separate school. You also might have attended a school in which you sat beside kids with disabilities. Your own schooling experience shapes your personal thoughts about inclusive education.

Before 1975, students with disabilities did not have the legal right to attend school. As a result, many students with more significant disabilities were educated in separate schools (paid for by their parents) or institutions or were not educated at all. In 1975, Congress passed the Education for All Handicapped Children Act (PL 94-142), which has since been reauthorized, most recently as the IDEA 2004 (PL 108-446). This law, which guarantees all students with disabilities the right to a public education, has proved a major step forward for people with disabilities and their families and has created the inclusion movement in the United States. In the years since 1975, when special education law went into effect, parents, advocates, and educators have worked to include one child at a time—fighting and planning child by child. The next step of this inclusion movement is creating authentically inclusive schools, and since the 1990s we have seen more schools create schoolwide systems to provide inclusive services to all students with disabilities in general education. We know this is possible and is done well in many places. We also know inclusive schools are not possible without leadership. IDEA 2004 ensures that all students with disabilities have access to FAPE in the LRE. Each of these terms is defined in the next section.

FREE APPROPRIATE PUBLIC EDUCATION

In order to explain what is meant by *free appropriate public education,* consider each term separately:

Free: All students with disabilities have the right to attend school, and the supports and services necessary to their education will be paid for at public expense.

Appropriate: All students with disabilities must be provided the assistive technology, aids, and services that allow them to participate in academic and nonacademic activities.

Public education: This education is guaranteed in a public school setting.

Least Restrictive Environment

The term that is used to support inclusion in the law is *LRE*. This term is explicitly cited in IDEA 2004 (PL 108-446), which stipulates that all students with disabilities have the legal right to be placed in the LRE.

LRE means that, to the maximum extent appropriate, a school district must educate any student with a disability in the regular classroom with appropriate aids and supports, referred to as *supplementary aids and services,* along with the student's peers without disabilities, in the school he or she would attend if the student did not have a disability (IDEA 2004).

Under LRE, the general education classroom is the first place to be considered for placing a student with a disability before more restrictive options are considered.

What Are Supplementary Aids and Services?

Supplementary aids and services that educators have successfully used include modifications to the regular class curriculum (e.g., preferential seating, use of a computer, taped lectures, reduced seat time), assistance of a teacher with special education training, special education training for the regular teacher, use of computer-assisted devices, provision of notetakers, and changes to materials. See Figure 3.1 for examples of supplementary aids and services.

Checklist of Sample Supplemental Supports, Aids, and Services

Directions: When considering the need for personalized supports, aids, or services for a student, use this checklist to help identify which supports will be the least intrusive, only as special as necessary, and the most natural to the context of the classroom.

Environmental	
	Preferential seating
	Planned seating ___ Bus ___ Classroom ___ Lunchroom ___ Auditorium ___ Other
	Alter physical room arrangement. (Specify:_____.)
	Use study carrels or quiet areas.
	Define area concretely (e.g., carpet squares, tape on floor, rug area).
	Reduce/minimize distractions. ___ Visual ___ Spatial ___ Auditory ___ Movement
	Teach positive rules for use of space.
Pacing of Instruction	
	Extend time requirements.
	Vary activity often.
	Allow breaks.
	Omit assignments requiring copying in timed situations.

Figure 3.1. Checklist of Sample Supplemental Supports, Aids, and Services. (*continued*)

Figure 3.1. *(continued)* (page 2 of 7)

	Send additional copy of the text home for summer preview.
	Provide home set of materials for preview or review.
Presentation of Subject Matter	
	Teach to the student's learning style/strength intelligences. ___ Verbal/Linguistic ___ Logical/Mathematical ___ Visual/Spatial ___ Naturalist ___ Bodily/Kinesthetic ___ Musical ___ Interpersonal ___ Intrapersonal
	Use active, experiential learning.
	Use specialized curriculum.
	Record class lectures and discussions to replay later.
	Use American Sign Language and/or total communication.
	Provide prewritten notes, an outline, or an organizer (e.g., mind map).
	Provide a copy of classmate's notes (e.g., use NCR paper, photocopy).
	Use functional and meaningful application of academic skills.
	Present demonstrations and models.
	Use manipulatives and real objects in mathematics.
	Highlight critical information or main ideas.
	Preteach vocabulary.
	Make and use vocabulary files or provide vocabulary lists.
	Reduce the language level of the reading assignment.
	Use facilitated communication.

(continued)

Republished with permission of Sage Publications, from Villa, R.A., Thousand, J.S., & Nevin, A.I. (2008). *A guide to co-teaching: Practical tips for facilitating learning* (2nd ed., pp. 169–171). Thousand Oaks, CA: Corwin Press; permission conveyed through Copyright Clearance Center, Inc.

In *The Principal's Handbook for Leading Inclusive Schools* by Julie Causton and George Theoharis
(2014, Paul H. Brookes Publishing Co., Inc.)

Figure 3.1.   *(continued)*   *(page 3 of 7)*

	Use visual organizers/sequences.
	Use paired reading/writing.
	Reduce seat time in class or activities.
	Use diaries or learning logs.
	Reword/rephrase instructions and questions.
	Preview and review major concepts in primary language.

Materials

	Limit amount of material on page.
	Record texts and other class materials.
	Use study guides and advanced organizers.
	Use supplementary materials.
	Provide note-taking assistance.
	Copy class notes.
	Scan tests and class notes into computer.
	Use large print.
	Use braille material.
	Use communication book or board.
	Provide assistive technology and software (e.g., Intelli-Talk).

Specialized Equipment or Procedure

	___ Wheelchair ___ Walker ___ Standing board ___ Positioning ___ Computer ___ Computer software ___ Electronic typewriter

(continued)

Republished with permission of Sage Publications, from Villa, R.A., Thousand, J.S., & Nevin, A.I. (2008). *A guide to co-teaching: Practical tips for facilitating learning* (2nd ed., pp. 169–171). Thousand Oaks, CA: Corwin Press; permission conveyed through Copyright Clearance Center, Inc.

In *The Principal's Handbook for Leading Inclusive Schools* by Julie Causton and George Theoharis
(2014, Paul H. Brookes Publishing Co., Inc.)

Figure 3.1. *(continued)* (page 4 of 7)

	___ Video
	___ Modified keyboard
	___ Voice synthesizer
	___ Switches
	___ Augmentative communication device
	___ Catheterization
	___ Suctioning
	___ Braces
	___ Restroom equipment
	___ Customized mealtime utensils, plates, cups, and other materials

Assignment Modification

	Give directions in small, distinct steps (written/picture/verbal).
	Use written backup for oral directions.
	Use pictures as supplement to oral directions. ___ Lower difficulty level. ___ Raise difficulty level. ___ Shorten assignments. ___ Reduce paper-and-pencil tasks.
	Read or record directions to the student(s).
	Give extra cues or prompts.
	Allow student to record or type assignments.
	Adapt worksheets and packets.
	Use compensatory procedures by providing alternate assignments, when demands of class conflict with student capabilities.
	Ignore spelling errors/sloppy work.
	Ignore penmanship.

Self-Management/Follow-Through

	Provide pictorial or written daily or weekly schedule.
	Provide student calendars.

(continued)

Republished with permission of Sage Publications, from Villa, R.A., Thousand, J.S., & Nevin, A.I. (2008). *A guide to co-teaching: Practical tips for facilitating learning* (2nd ed., pp. 169–171). Thousand Oaks, CA: Corwin Press; permission conveyed through Copyright Clearance Center, Inc.

In *The Principal's Handbook for Leading Inclusive Schools* by Julie Causton and George Theoharis
(2014, Paul H. Brookes Publishing Co., Inc.)

Figure 3.1. *(continued)*   *(page 5 of 7)*

	Check often for understanding/review.
	Request parent reinforcement.
	Have student repeat directions.
	Teach study skills.
	Use binders to organize material.
	Design/write/use long-term assignment time lines.
	Review and practice real situations.
	Plan for generalization by teaching skill in several environments.

Testing Adaptations

	Provide oral instructions and/or read test questions.
	Use pictorial instructions/questions.
	Read test to student.
	Preview language of test questions.
	Ask questions that have applications in real settings.
	Administer test individually. ___ Use short answer. ___ Use multiple choice. ___ Shorten length. ___ Extend time frame. ___ Use open-note/open-book tests.
	Modify format to reduce visual complexity or confusion.

Social Interaction Support

	Use natural peer supports and multiple, rotating peers.
	Use peer advocacy.
	Use cooperative learning group.

(continued)

Figure 3.1. *(continued)* *(page 6 of 7)*

	Institute peer tutoring.
	Structure opportunities for social interaction (e.g., Circle of Friends).
	Focus on social process rather than end product.
	Structure shared experiences in school and extracurricular activities.
	Teach friendship, sharing, and negotiation skills to classmates.
	Teach social communication skills. ___ Greetings ___ Conversation ___ Turn Taking ___ Sharing ___ Negotiation ___ Other

Level of Staff Support (Consider *after* considering previous categories)

	Consultation
	Stop-in support
	Team teaching (parallel, supportive, complementary, or co-teaching)
	Daily in-class staff support
	Total staff support (staff are in close proximity)
	One-to-one assistance
	Specialized personnel support (if indicated, identify time needed)

Support		**Time Needed**
	Instructional support assistant	
	Health care assistant	
	Behavior assistant	

(continued)

Republished with permission of Sage Publications, from Villa, R.A., Thousand, J.S., & Nevin, A.I. (2008). *A guide to co-teaching: Practical tips for facilitating learning* (2nd ed., pp. 169–171). Thousand Oaks, CA: Corwin Press; permission conveyed through Copyright Clearance Center, Inc.

In *The Principal's Handbook for Leading Inclusive Schools* by Julie Causton and George Theoharis
(2014, Paul H. Brookes Publishing Co., Inc.)

Figure 3.1. *(continued)* *(page 7 of 7)*

	Signing assistant	
	Nursing	
	Occupational therapy	
	Physical therapy	
	Speech-language pathologist	
	Augmentative communication specialist	
	Transportation	
	Counseling	
	Adaptive physical education	
	Transition planning	
	Orientation/mobility	
	Career counseling	

In *The Principal's Handbook for Leading Inclusive Schools* by Julie Causton and George Theoharis
(2014, Paul H. Brookes Publishing Co., Inc.)

Educators must utilize all of the possible supplementary aids and services before determining that a student can leave the general education classroom. Inclusion is not mentioned in the law, but it is implied, and people use LRE and the multitude of supplementary aids and services to support the idea of inclusion. Therefore, inclusion has been defined by scholars.

DEFINING INCLUSIVE EDUCATION

Kunc defined *inclusive education* as

> The valuing of diversity within the human community. When inclusive education is fully embraced, we abandon the idea that children have to become "normal" in order to contribute to the world. . . . We begin to look beyond typical ways of becoming valued members of the community, and in doing so, begin to realize the achievable goal of providing all children with an authentic sense of belonging. (1992, p. 20)

Udvari-Solner used another definition of inclusion:

> Inclusive schooling propels a critique of contemporary school culture and thus, encourages practitioners to reinvent what can be and should be to realize more humane, just and democratic learning communities. Inequities in treatment and educational opportunity are brought to the forefront, thereby fostering attention to human rights, respect for difference and value of diversity. (1997, p. 142)

WHAT DOES INCLUSION LOOK LIKE? INDICATORS OF INCLUSIVE CLASSROOMS

Some of the indicators of good inclusive education include utilizing natural proportions, team teaching, building community, differentiation, students remaining in the classroom, and engaging instruction. Each of these indicators is described below.

Natural Proportions

In any one classroom, the number of students with disabilities should reflect the natural population of students with disabilities in the school (i.e., no more than 12%). In an inclusive classroom, half the class will not be made up of students with disabilities. Having a greater number of students with disabilities in one setting increases the density of need, making the class more like a special education setting. As a principal, this concept is critical, because the principal often is involved in helping to create schedules for students and for placing students into classrooms.

Team Teaching

Inclusive classrooms often have two teachers (one general and one special education teacher) with equitable responsibilities for teaching all the students. A paraprofessional often provides additional support to the students who have disabilities while also working with all students in the classroom.

Community Building

In inclusive classrooms, teachers continually use community building to ensure that students feel connected to one another and to their teachers. A common theme in community building is that different people learn in different ways. Community building approaches vary, but, in an inclusive classroom, the day may start out with a morning meeting at which students share their feelings or important life events. Organized community building may occur in which students learn about each other in systematic ways. For example, the students might be doing a community building exercise called "Homework in a Bag"; in this exercise, each student brings one item that represents him- or herself and shares the item with a small group of other students.

Differentiation

In an inclusive classroom, it is clear that learners of various academic, social, and behavioral levels and needs share one learning environment. Therefore, the content is differentiated. Students might work on similar goals, but they do so in different ways. For example, all students might be working on math problems, with some using manipulatives, some drawing out their answers, some checking their problems on calculators, and some using wipe-off markers and white boards.

Students Do Not Leave to Learn

An inclusive classroom does not have a virtual revolving door of children leaving for specialized instruction. Therapies and services occur within the context of the general education classroom. For example, instead of going to a small room with a speech teacher, a student works on his or her speech goals while participating in reading instruction.

Engaging Instruction

Inclusive classrooms do not entail a lot of large-group lectures in which the teachers talk and the students passively sit and listen. Learning is exciting in inclusive classrooms. Teachers plan instruction with the range of learning styles in mind. In inclusive classrooms, students experience active learning; they often are up and out of their seats, with partner work and group work used frequently. The content is planned to meet the needs of students to move around, to work with others, and to experience their learning.

HOW DOES INCLUSIVE EDUCATION FIT WITH RESPONSE TO INTERVENTION?

Many schools and districts across the country have adopted the tiered response to intervention (RTI) model, often presented in the form of a triangle: the base of the triangle is good curriculum and instruction, then some students are given prescribed intervention, and fewer students receive additional and even more focused intervention. Seen within the context of the RTI and PBS triangles, authentic inclusive education is a way to significantly expand the base of the triangle to allow many students who typically struggle in that base to be more successful. It is important to recognize that the schools that embrace inclusive education are seeing positive results for students who typically receive interventions in more restrictive settings.

In practice, RTI seeks to remediate skills for "at risk" students' so-called deficiencies by changing the intensity of intervention (i.e., explicit instruction, increased frequency, lengthened duration, homogeneous groups created) (Ferri, 2011). This practice promotes assimilation. It is important to be careful in adopting RTI, as we have seen over and over that within a move to RTI the general education curriculum is not revised, or other instructional strategies are not integrated to meet students' needs. Instead, data on the irresponsiveness to intervention is documented and students are still seen as deficient. There is danger to this, for if the school sees the "problem" or deficiency as lying within the student, staff are less likely to modify and differentiate teaching and curriculum than if they saw the "problem" as a mismatch between the student's and the school's learning environments, the way classrooms run, and the kinds of instructional approaches used.

Whereas some schools are looking for the prescriptive intervention to be delivered to a targeted group of students, inclusive education can offer a way to provide more seamless and integrated support. Schools that embrace inclusion are improving the way they meet all students' needs within the context of the general education setting through community building and differentiation, thereby giving students access to a rich social environment and the academic core curriculum.

WHAT DO I NEED TO KNOW ABOUT THE INDIVIDUALIZED EDUCATION PROGRAM?

Every student who receives special education services must have an IEP. A student who has an IEP has already been tested and observed, and a team has determined that the student has a disability. An IEP is a legal plan written by a team of professionals that documents the learning priorities for the school year (Huefner, 2000). This team includes the parent, the student (when appropriate), the general education teacher, the special education teacher, a representative of the school district, and other professionals whose expertise is needed (e.g., psychologist, SLP, OT, PT). When writing this document, the team comes together annually to determine and document the student's unique needs and goals regarding his or her participation in the general school curriculum for the upcoming school year. According to the U.S. Department of Education (2004), every IEP must legally include the following information:

- Present levels of performance—this states how a student is performing across all subject areas.

- Measurable goals and objectives—this indicates the annual goals for a student across subject areas.

- Special education and related services—this is the type, level, and amount of service that will be provided by special education staff.

- The extent of participation with children without disabilities—the IEP must note how much time a student spends with general education peers.

- A statement of how the child's progress will be measured—the team needs to describe how often and how a student's progress will be measured.

- Modifications—the student's modifications or adaptations must be listed.

- Participation in statewide tests—the IEP indicates whether the student will participate in statewide tests and, if so, what modifications will be provided.

- Locations of services to be provided—this explains the amount of time students will receive services and the location (e.g., general education classroom).

- Statement of transition services—each student who is at least 16 years of age must have a statement of preparation for adult life.

The principal can serve as the local educational agency (LEA) representative in IEP meetings, overseeing the process of the construction of the IEP. In addition, the principal may be required to make decisions that relate to finances. For example, if a parent requests a paraprofessional for their son or daughter, the principal would help to determine if it is necessary, because that request has financial implications. Table 3.2 provides a guide to reading an IEP. When reading an IEP, the best place to start is with two major sections: 1) the present level of performance and 2) the student's goals and objectives. When reading an IEP, fill out an "IEP at a glance" or a summary listing the goals and objectives and other important information. See Figure 3.2 for a copy of an IEP at a glance. You should understand that the information within the document is confidential and cannot be shared with anyone outside of the child's team. Sharing information about a student is not only disrespectful; it is also potentially illegal (20 U.S.C. § 1412 [a][8]; § 1417 [c]).

Any student who has challenging behavior is required to have a behavior intervention plan as part of the IEP. This plan includes a functional assessment of the student's behavior and a plan for addressing that student's behavior in positive ways. If a student has a behavior intervention plan, the school principal and staff are responsible for following the behavior plan as written.

Table 3.2. How to read an individualized education program

1. Find the present level of performance. Read it. Now ask yourself…	Do I have a clear picture of what this student does well?
	Do I have a clear picture of this student's skills?
	Do I know any strategies that work with this student?
	Do I know what to avoid when working with this student?
2. Find the annual goals. Read each goal. Now ask yourself…	Do I have a clear picture of what the student should be able to do by the end of the year?
3. Find the supplementary aids and services (aids, services, and supports to help the student be educated in the general education environment). Read it. Now ask yourself…	Do I understand the services and supports that this student needs in regular education environments?
	Do I know who is expected to provide the services or supports?
	If I am expected to provide a service or support, do I know what to do?
4. Find the section on specially designed instruction (direct teaching and services carried out by the special education staff). Read it. Now ask yourself…	What specially designed instruction does this student need?
	Where is the instruction provided?
	If I am expected to provide practice or support, do I understand what to do?
5. If the student has a behavior intervention plan, find it. Read it. Ask yourself…	What are the strategies and techniques that will increase the likelihood that appropriate behaviors will occur?
	If problem behaviors begin to escalate, how can I redirect the student to more positive behaviors?
	If the student becomes aggressive, do I know the steps in the response plan to de-escalate the situation?
6. Now read the rest of the individualized education program. Ask yourself…	Do I have any questions about this student, his or her needs, or his or her support that I should share with my teaching team?

COMMONLY ASKED QUESTIONS ABOUT INCLUSIVE EDUCATION

Q. Is inclusive education really best for a particular student?

A. This question is common to teachers and paraprofessionals alike. Their job is to figure out how to make the general education environment suitable to the student's needs.

Q. A teacher reports that his or her student "isn't getting anything out of the class" and wants to place that student in a segregated classroom. What should the principal do?

A. It is the teacher's responsibility (under the principal's leadership) to modify or adapt the content so that the student can benefit from the instruction. Sometimes, the goals of the lesson are not easy to see. In such cases, the principal

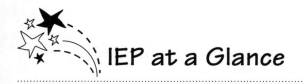

IEP at a Glance

....

Student:_____ **Grade:**_____ **Age:**_____

Date completed: _____	
Goal: _____	**Goal:** _____
Objectives: • • •	**Objectives:** • • •
Goal: _____	**Goal:** _____
Objectives: • • •	**Objectives:** • • •
Goal: _____	**Goal:** _____
Objectives: • • •	**Objectives:** • • •

Important student information:
•
•
•
•
•
•
•
•

Figure 3.2. Individualized Education Program (IEP) at a Glance.

should initiate a discussion with the teacher(s) about what the expected goals of the lesson are (the student might be working on social goals, occupational therapy goals, or just being present to learn the content).

Q. A parent has called because another student makes noise in the classroom and it is bothering his or her child. When should a student be taken out of the classroom?

A. Some students make noises during class or distract other students. Most of these behaviors are attempts to communicate or the result of disabilities. There are significant problems with reacting by removing a child. Think how you would feel if you were removed from a learning environment; you might feel angry, humiliated, or embarrassed. Students have the same reaction. If such actions are used continually, a student might begin to feel that something is wrong with him or her. Removing a student can create an environment that feels unsafe. Every student has the right to an education in the general education classroom, but care must be taken if other students are becoming too distracted. If a student is having behavioral issues, the team of teachers has the responsibility to identify and help the student manage the behavior within the context of the classroom. The student can be given an option to identify when he or she might need a break.

Q. What could a teacher do instead of removing a student?

A. The teacher could try leaving the situation. Sometimes, switching adults or backing away is the best solution if a teacher is having a difficult time with a student. Also, the student can be helped to engage in a different way, or given a choice at a difficult moment (e.g., a choice of materials, a choice of whom to work with). The school leadership should see removal as the last resort. Chapter 8 presents many more ideas for managing behavioral issues.

Q. Will other kids tease students with disabilities?

A. If the principal sees or hears about teasing, he or she must deal with it immediately. Teasing should not be seen as an inevitable consequence of inclusion. In fact, in inclusive settings, teasing often is not an issue, but if it becomes one, it must be dealt with directly and swiftly.

Q. Is inclusion really the law?

A. IDEA 2004 does not use the term *inclusion*. Nonetheless, the law stipulates that all students must be placed in the LRE. The first consideration must be the general education setting, and schools must prove that they have attempted to teach all children in the general education setting with appropriate supplementary aids and services before considering placement in more restrictive settings.

CONCLUSION

Schools today are becoming increasingly inclusive, and principals need to lead the charge. Therefore, it is important to understand the rationale for inclusive schooling, the history of inclusive schooling, major concepts in inclusive schooling, indicators of inclusion, and the concept of the IEP as a framework to most fully support students in inclusive settings. Though you will be leading the charge, you will not be expected to do this alone, but rather as you lead part of a school team. The next chapter focuses on how the principal fits into a collaborative team that will work to educate all students.

NOTES

4

Leading Inclusive School Reform

A TALE OF TWO SCHOOLS.

"We argue that a school cannot be a social justice school, a high achieving school, a successful school . . . unless the school has also eliminated segregated pullout programs."

—Frattura and Capper (2007)

In Chapter 1, we argued that principals are instrumental figures in creating and carrying out a vision for inclusive schools. Each year since 1974, when students with disabilities were guaranteed the right to a free and appropriate public education, more students with disabilities have been educated in general education schools and classrooms (Data Accountability Center, 2010; U.S. Department of Education, 2009). Inclusion has evolved over time and, increasingly, schools are giving students with disabilities access to rich academic instruction, connection to their peers, and full membership in their schools and communities. This evolution, in conjunction with the new era of standards in which schools and districts are being held increasingly accountable for the achievement of students with disabilities, has created the need to focus on leadership for inclusion with regard to special education.

In this era of standards and accountability, a key aspect in thinking about the achievement of students with disabilities is the idea of access—access to general education curriculum (which directly relates to the content of standardized tests), access to high-quality instruction, and access to peers (the social and emotional aspects of schooling). Since students with disabilities gained the right to public education, scholars have developed a compelling body of literature documenting the impact of inclusive services for students with disabilities (see Peterson & Hittie, 2009, for a listing of many of these studies). More recently, Cosier (2010) examined a national database and found that, for every additional hour students with disabilities spend in general education, there is a significant gain of achievement across all disabilities categories. Thus, it is of great importance to maximize the access to general education of all students with disabilities. This chapter focuses on how leaders transform their current school into inclusive schools for all students—inclusive school reform.

To understand this transformation, we rely on the research examining the role that leaders play in creating inclusive schools for students with disabilities (see Capper, Frattura, & Keyes, 2000; Capper & Frattura, 2008; McLesky & Waldron, 2002; Riehl, 2000; Theoharis, 2009). In examining this work and from our experience working with many schools and districts to accomplish this, a number of key ideas emerge that inform the practice of inclusive school reform. School leaders successful at creating inclusive schools take on a variety of strategies in this work. These include 1) setting a vision, 2) developing democratic implementation plans, 3) using staff (teachers and paraprofessionals) in systematic ways to create inclusive service delivery, 4) creating and developing teams that work collaboratively to meet the range of student needs, 5) providing ongoing learning opportunities for staff, 6) monitoring and adjusting the service delivery each year, and 7) purposefully working to develop a climate of belonging for students and staff. The framework for inclusive reform presented in this chapter is built upon this foundational research and practice.

INCLUSIVE SCHOOL REFORM

Inclusive school reform has resulted in all students with disabilities being placed into general education settings (including students with significant disabilities, students with mild disabilities, students with emotional disabilities, students with autism . . . all students) and providing inclusive services to meet their needs while eliminating pullout or self-contained special education programs. In the following subsections, we outline a seven-part process. This process is adapted from the Planning Alternative Tomorrows with Hope (PATH) planning process (Pearpoint, O'Brien, & Forest, 1993). See Figure 4.1, the Inclusive School Reform Planning Tool. It is important that the steps in the inclusive reform process are carried out in a democratic and transparent manner. We recommend that a representative leadership team consisting of school administrators, general education teachers, special education teachers, and other staff members go through this process together. It is also important for this team to check in and communicate with the entire staff throughout the process.

Step 1—Setting a Vision

First, the team sets a vision for the school reform initiative (Step 1 on the Inclusive School Reform Planning Tool, Figure 4.1) around three areas: 1) school structure (i.e., how we arrange adults and students), 2) meeting the needs of all in general education, and 3) school climate. Many schools have gone through this process already; we provide an example of goals that a K–8 school created during its inclusive school reform work:

Structure Goals (how we arrange adults and students)

- Students will be placed in balanced classrooms with positive role models.

- The designated person will facilitate efficient monthly communication meetings for staff to discuss various topics surrounding inclusion.

School Climate Goals

- Examine the physical structure to determine locations conducive to planning, supporting, and implementing inclusion at each grade level.

- Create a schedule that promotes consistent and common planning time for ongoing communication and dialogue.

- Develop and implement approaches and procedures that promote a professional learning community (e.g., collaboration, consensus, agree to disagree respectfully).

Meeting the Needs of All in the General Education Classroom Goals

- Have planned opportunities for vertical communication to provide continuity between grade levels.

- Provide child-centered, differentiated, research-based instruction that challenges children of all abilities, supported by targeted staff development.

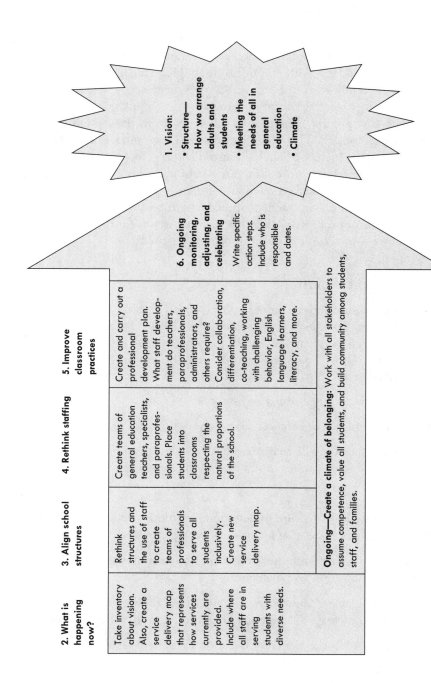

Figure 4.1. Inclusive School Reform Planning Tool. (*Source:* Pearpoint, O'Brien, & Forest, 1993.)

Step 2—What Is Happening Now?
Creating Service Delivery Maps

For the second step, we recommend that the leadership team examine the existing way special education services are provided, the way human resources are used, and other important data. This process requires school teams to map out their current service delivery and the way they use their human resources in efforts to meet the range of student needs. In order for the team to understand the current service delivery and to be able to discuss it together, it is necessary to create a visual representation of the classrooms, special education service providers, general education classrooms, and how students receive their related services. An essential part of creating a service map is to indicate which staff pull students from which classrooms, which students learn in self-contained spaces, which paraprofessionals are used where—a complete picture of how and where all staff at the school work.

Figure 4.2 provides an example of this kind of visual map of the service delivery model at an elementary school before inclusive school reform. The rectangles around the edges represent the general education classrooms. The ovals in the middle labeled *Resource* represent resource special education teachers who worked with students with disabilities from many classrooms (as indicated by the arrows) through a pullout model. The circle labeled *Self-contained* represents a multi-age group of students with

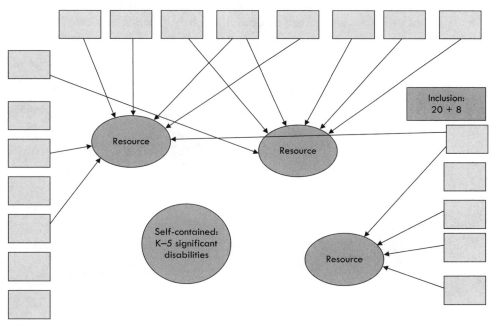

Figure 4.2. Special education service delivery *before* inclusive reform. (*Note:* Rectangles, elementary general education classrooms K–5. Ovals, special education teachers. Resource, a special education teacher who pulls students from the general education classroom. Inclusion: 20 + 8, a classroom where a general education teacher is team teaching with a special education teacher, with 20 general education students and 8 special education students. Self-contained: K–5 significant disabilities, a special education classroom where all students who have significant disabilities receive their instruction and spend the majority of their school day.) (Reprinted by permission of the Publisher. From George Theoharis, <u>The School Leaders Our Children Deserve</u>, New York: Teachers College Press. Copyright © 2009 by Teachers College, Columbia University. All rights reserved.)

disabilities who spent the entire day together, separate from general education peers. One rectangle is marked with *Inclusion: 20 + 8*. This represents what was previously called an "inclusive" classroom. This room had about 20 general education students with an additional eight students with disabilities.

This old service delivery plan concentrated or overloaded intense needs into certain classrooms; other classrooms lacked both students with disabilities and additional adult support. The visual representation captures the way special education teachers were providing support. As you can see, in this model some students were excluded and removed from the general education curriculum, instruction, and social interaction with general education peers for some or all of each school day.

Step 3—Align School Structures

Step 3 involves rethinking structures and the use of staff in order to create teams of professionals to serve all students inclusively—in other words, creating a new service delivery map. After creating a map of the current service delivery, the staff works to create a new inclusive service delivery plan by redeploying staff to make balanced and heterogeneous classrooms where all students are included in order to enhance inclusion and belonging. Figure 4.3 provides an example of inclusive service delivery.

The new service delivery shown in Figure 4.3 was created by the same school depicted in Figure 4.2. Teachers and administrators reconfigured the use of staff to form teams of specialists and general education teachers to create inclusive teams that

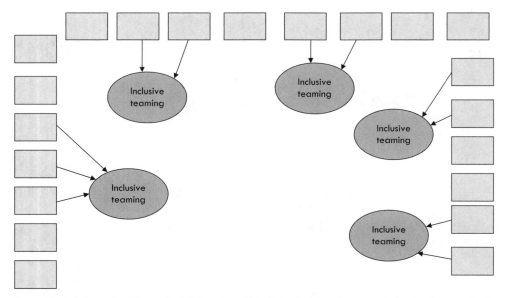

Figure 4.3. Inclusive service delivery *after* inclusive reform. (*Note:* Rectangles, elementary general education classrooms. Ovals, special education teachers. Inclusive teaming, a special education teacher teaming with two to three regular education teachers to meet the range of student needs within the classroom. Each team has one paraprofessional assigned as well.) (Reprinted by permission of the Publisher. From George Theoharis, <u>The School Leaders Our Children Deserve,</u> New York: Teachers College Press. Copyright © 2009 by Teachers College, Columbia University. All rights reserved.)

collaboratively plan and deliver instruction to heterogeneous student groups. In this example, the school chose to pair special education teachers as part of inclusive teams with two to three general education classrooms and teachers. It is important to note that no new resources or staff were added to become fully inclusive: if a school builds inclusive service delivery using additional resources, if and when those resources go away, the plan will fall apart. We recognize that every school leadership team wishes it had more resources and more staff to support students. However, it is essential to build the inclusive service delivery with the current resources and staffing.

It is also tempting for some to try to maintain separate programs. For example, one school tried to move toward inclusive services while maintaining its self-contained programs. This resulted in staff being stretched too thin, with some students still being excluded and some being overloaded into certain classrooms. The school leadership realized that they needed to use all of their teachers to make a fully inclusive plan, and for the following year changed their plan. This reminds us that we need to use all of the resources at our disposal to create the new inclusive service delivery and not attempt to keep some students and therefore some resources separate.

Step 4—Rethink Staffing: Creating Instructional Teams

The fourth step in the process is to rethink the use of staff. This involves creating teams of general education teachers, specialists (e.g., special education teachers, teachers for English language learners [ELLs], others), and paraprofessionals to serve all students inclusively. In the school depicted in Figures 4.2 and 4.3, the special education teacher who was formerly a teacher in the self-contained classroom (Figure 4.2) now is co-teaching and co-planning with two general education teachers (Figure 4.3) and a paraprofessional. Chapter 5 of this book focuses specifically on the collaboration of these teams.

An essential component of this step is placing students into classrooms using the school's natural proportions of students with special education needs or other needs (like ELLs) as a guide. This means that if 13% of the students at the school have disabilities, then the student placement process should mirror that density of students with special needs in each classroom and not create classrooms with high percentages of students with special needs. Part of the task of creating classes for any age group—whether at elementary, middle, or high school—is to not overload or cluster many students with special education needs into one room or section. Using natural proportions as a guide, it is important to strive for balanced or heterogeneous classes that mix abilities, achievement, behavior, and other learning needs.

Step 5—Improving Classroom Practices

For the fifth step, it is important to change the daily classroom practices that the newly created teaching teams will use. This involves creating and carrying out a professional development plan for teachers, paraprofessionals, and administrators. We recommend that schools consider such topics as collaboration, co-teaching, differentiated instruction, working with challenging behavior, inquiry-based instruction, ELL methods, and literacy. In our experience, all the schools that have become more inclusive through this process have spent significant professional development time and energy learning about collaboration, co-teaching, and differentiation. See Figure 4.4 for a useful form for providing teams with feedback about the classroom environment. Chapters 7 and 8 in this book focus on how leaders can have an impact on classroom practices in academics and behavior.

Step 6—Ongoing Monitoring, Adjusting, and Celebrating

The sixth component of the inclusive reform process is to monitor and adjust the plan, getting feedback from all staff, students, and families, but without abandoning the plan at the first moment of struggle or resistance. During the summer and into the first few weeks of the year, it is important to iron out logistics and adjust teaching schedules as needed. Then, to continue monitoring and adjusting, the leadership team begins to plan for the following year midway through each school year. In addition, this component involves making time to honor the hard work of school reform—specifically, the new roles and responsibilities that teaching teams have had to adopt—and celebrating successes along the way. Schools going through this process have done a variety of things to this end: mid-fall celebrations for staff to keep momentum, banner-raising celebrations to declare a commitment to this effort while inviting local officials and the press, and end of the year celebrations to finish the year on a positive note.

Step 7—Ongoing: Create a Climate of Belonging

An ongoing part of inclusive reform needs to be creating a climate of belonging. A component of this necessitates involving all staff in the planning and implementation of the inclusive reform. Also, creating a climate of belonging means working with all stakeholders at school to assume competence and to value all students, building community purposefully in each classroom throughout the year, adopting a school-wide community-building approach, and enhancing the sense of belonging for all students, staff, and families. See Figure 4.5 for an observation form to help provide staff with feedback about issues of belonging.

It is important to note that the research and our experience with this process suggest that all seven aspects are needed. We recommend that implementation of reformed inclusive service delivery happens between Steps 4 and 5.

IMPLICATIONS FOR DISTRICTS

The steps described in the preceding section detail how to create inclusive schooling at the school level; however, many district administrators inquire about how to create an entirely inclusive district. Some district administrators engage in the seven-step inclusive school reform process on a school-by-school basis. Others undertake a large-scale approach. Figure 4.6 outlines some guidelines to use when moving an entire district to greater inclusion and points out common pitfalls.

Classroom Environment Feedback Form

		Date:	Time:
Lesson/content:		**Teachers:** 1. 2.	
		Other adults present:	

	Look for:	Evidence:	Descriptions:
Seating arrangements	Students with disabilities are not all seated together.	❑ Not evident ❑ Emerging ❑ Evident ❑ Much evidence	Where are students with disabilities seated?
	Students are provided with choices in where they are seated.	❑ Not evident ❑ Emerging ❑ Evident ❑ Much evidence	
	All students are equally spaced throughout the classroom.	❑ Not evident ❑ Emerging ❑ Evident ❑ Much evidence	What types of seating arrangements are used throughout the lesson?
Student ownership	Student work and art are displayed throughout the classroom.	❑ Not evident ❑ Emerging ❑ Evident ❑ Much evidence	What do the walls of the classroom look like?
	Student-written rules, calendars, agendas, and so forth are present in the classroom.	❑ Not evident ❑ Emerging ❑ Evident ❑ Much evidence	In what other ways is student pride evident in the classroom?

Figure 4.4.   Classroom Environment Feedback Form.

(continued)

Figure 4.4. *(continued)* (page 2 of 2)

Organizing the space	Quiet areas are available for students.	❑ Not evident ❑ Emerging ❑ Evident ❑ Much evidence	Where are these located and what materials are in that space?
	The classroom space is divided up by learning activity.	❑ Not evident ❑ Emerging ❑ Evident ❑ Much evidence	What learning activities do students engage in throughout different parts of the room?
	Designated space exists for students to engage in movement.	❑ Not evident ❑ Emerging ❑ Evident ❑ Much evidence	What sensory materials are in this space?
Materials and accommodations	Teachers provide all students with necessary materials.	❑ Not evident ❑ Emerging ❑ Evident ❑ Much evidence	What materials are used and are they adapted for student needs?
	Students have easy access to their accommodations and communication devices.	❑ Not evident ❑ Emerging ❑ Evident ❑ Much evidence	What accommodations are used and what communication devices are present in the classroom?
Adult language and tone	Teachers use language and tone that is positive and respectful toward students.	❑ Not evident ❑ Emerging ❑ Evident ❑ Much evidence	What kinds of verbal interactions take place?
	Teachers use language and tone that is professional and respectful with other adults.	❑ Not evident ❑ Emerging ❑ Evident ❑ Much evidence	What kinds of verbal interactions take place about and between adults?

Comments: _____

_____

_____

_____

_____

Belonging Feedback Form

	Date:	Time:
Lesson/content:	**Teachers:**	
	1.	
	2.	
	Other adults present:	

	Look for:	Evidence:	Descriptions:
Friendships	Teachers facilitate classroom friendships.	❏ Not evident ❏ Emerging ❏ Evident ❏ Much evidence	What strategies do the teachers use to facilitate friendships?
	Friendships throughout the classroom are evident regardless of disability label.	❏ Not evident ❏ Emerging ❏ Evident ❏ Much evidence	What kinds of friendships exist?
Student interaction	Teachers use cooperative learning strategies.	❏ Not evident ❏ Emerging ❏ Evident ❏ Much evidence	What strategies are implemented?
	Students interact with a variety of other students in the classroom.	❏ Not evident ❏ Emerging ❏ Evident ❏ Much evidence	What kinds of interactions occur?
Peer support	Teachers provide opportunities for students to tutor and mentor each other.	❏ Not evident ❏ Emerging ❏ Evident ❏ Much evidence	Where are these located and what materials are in that space?
	Students are taught and supported by peers.	❏ Not evident ❏ Emerging ❏ Evident ❏ Much evidence	What learning activities do students engage in throughout different parts of the room?

Figure 4.5. Belonging Feedback Form.

(continued)

Figure 4.5. *(continued)* (page 2 of 2)

Classroom community	Teachers employ a democratic curriculum.	❏ Not evident ❏ Emerging ❏ Evident ❏ Much evidence	How are issues of social justice reflected in the lesson?
	Students engage in community-building activities.	❏ Not evident ❏ Emerging ❏ Evident ❏ Much evidence	What community-building activities are used?

Comments: _____

_____

_____

_____

_____

District/School Inclusive Placement Guidelines

The following guidelines are for administrators to use when making student placement decisions and policies. While not exhaustive, they represent a range of key decisions that can foster inclusion, belonging, and learning.

These guidelines can be used to avoid common administrative pitfalls that set up structures impeding achievement and creating seclusion. They are not meant to be a recipe, but are intended to help put structures and policies in place to create truly inclusive schools.

Home district: All students are educated within their school district.

No students (including, e.g., students with significant disabilities, students with challenging behaviors, students with autism) are sent to other districts or cooperative programs outside of the home school district.

Home school: All students attend the schools and classrooms they would attend regardless of ability or disability or native language.

No schools within the district are set aside for students with disabilities.

General education member: All students are placed in chronologically age-appropriate *general education classrooms.*

This is a legal entitlement, not based on staff preference or comfort level. Each classroom represents a heterogeneous group of students. Special education is a service, not a place. No programs, schools-within-a-school, or classrooms are set aside for students with disabilities. Students with disabilities are not slotted into predetermined programs, schools, or classrooms. Particular classrooms are not designated as inclusive classrooms while others are not.

Density check: Strive for classroom sections that represent natural proportions of the school building.

Natural proportions refers to the percentage of students with disabilities in the student body. If you have 10 students with disabilities and 100 students in the school, that natural proportion is 10 percent. The national average of students with disabilities is 12 percent.

Special education teachers' caseloads: Assignment of students with disabilities balances the intensity of student need and case-management responsibility.

This balance moves away from certain special educators being the "inclusive," "resource," "self-contained" or "emotionally disturbed" teachers to all special educators having similar roles and caseloads. Students with disabilities with similar labels are not clustered together.

Team arrangements: All teachers (e.g., general education, special education, English language learner, reading) are assigned to instructional teams on the basis of shared students.

Special education teachers are assigned to collaborate with two or three classroom sections or teachers to promote collaboration, communication, and co-planning. Creating effective teams of adults who work with the same students is essential; consider grouping compatible adult team members as well as building the capacity in all staff members to work with all students. Professional development is needed for adults to embrace these new roles, collaborate well, and effectively use meeting time.

Related services: Related services are portable services that come to the student.

Therefore, related service teachers consult with classroom teams, demonstrate skills and techniques, and provide instruction and/or support within the context of general education. Related service providers need to be a part of the process of placing students into general education classrooms and of the daily general education planning and program.

Daily schedule: Use the schedule to support instructional blocks, time for collaborative planning and problem solving, and daily direction and training for paraprofessionals.

The master schedule is used as a tool to leverage the vision of collaborative inclusion. Creating sacred planning time for teams of general educators and special educators is essential.

Service delivery teams: District and school-level teams meet regularly to reconfigure resources and to revise service delivery on an annual basis.

Schools engage in an ongoing process to plan for the specific needs of their students. This involves re-examining the current way in which staff are used, how teams are created, the class placement process, and the master schedule.

Figure 4.6. District/school guidelines for inclusive student placement.

COMMONLY ASKED QUESTIONS ABOUT SCHOOL REFORM

Q. I recognize we need to be more inclusive, but I think my staff needs to build their skills to meet the range of learners' needs and in general become more effective first. Should we engage in that professional learning first?

A. We have seen many schools try this approach to improve in general before including all students. This has proven largely unsuccessful as most of the time the staff never "improves enough" and still does not feel they have the skills to include all students. This approach also leaves the step of actually including students as off in the future and given the frequent changes in school leaders and priorities, this then rarely happens. We do not recommend this approach. However, if it must be taken, we recommend committing to a time line of not more than 1 year before including all students.

Q. Would it be better to take one grade level at a time and slowly move into inclusion?

A. We have experienced this approach as well and we have two major concerns with it. First, it takes years and years before all students are included by building a program one grade at a time (i.e., at a K–8 school it would take 9 years). Second, this slow pace often acts as a barrier for full implementation as leaders change, priorities change, staff can create additional barriers to advancing inclusion, and momentum dies. We do not recommend this approach.

Q. Would it be better to just start with volunteer teachers and let the rest of the staff see how inclusion can happen?

A. It makes a lot of sense to harness the energy advantage of enthusiastic teachers and teams of professionals who want to work together. This is rarely enough to include all students, so it relegates inclusive services to some students in pockets of the school. It then rarely spreads to the entire school and this allows some staff who do not volunteer to maintain the erroneous belief that they are not teachers for students with disabilities.

Q. In moving toward more inclusive services, would it make sense to use some of my special education staff to do pullout interventions or functional skills/self-contained programming for students with significant needs?

A. We strongly recommend that in moving to inclusive services it becomes a school-wide philosophy and that all resources (namely special education staff and general education staff) are used to build collaborative teams to inclusively meet the needs of all students. We have seen schools move toward inclusion but keep some special education teachers to run separate programs and pullout services. This leaves the teachers who are working to include students spread too thin and creates fragmented service delivery. We do not recommend this as this approach does not harness all of the available human resources to make effective inclusive services efficient and not spread teams too thin. Maintaining reasonable numbers of general education teachers for special education teachers to co-plan and teach with requires putting the maximum resources (all staff) toward this endeavor.

CONCLUSION

This chapter focused on the process and leadership involved in inclusive school reform for students with disabilities. It is important to note that students with disabilities historically and currently are not the only subset of students who have been systematically denied access to the general education classroom. Students of color and low-income students (due to overrepresentation in special education and a reliance on more restrictive placements), students learning English as a second language, students who receive related services, and students who have behavioral issues are much more likely to experience exclusion from the general education curriculum, instruction, and peers. The most important thing to note here is that access to the general education core curriculum is paramount.

When students are removed from the general education classroom for any type of service, there is a tradeoff and cost to that. Students miss important content and fall further behind. Inclusive school reform, when done correctly, looks not only at students with disabilities, but also at all other groups of marginalized students, and prioritizes full-time access to the general education curriculum, instruction, and peer groups. The focus is on seamlessly providing students the services and supports that they need within the context of general education in order for all students to reach their social and academic potentials.

NOTES

5

The Backbone of Inclusion

Leading Effective Collaboration

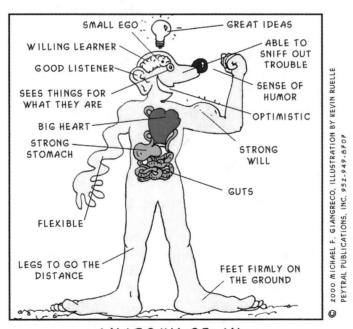

ANATOMY OF AN
EFFECTIVE TEAM MEMBER

"Getting teams of general educators and special educators to work well together to co-plan and co-deliver instruction is what makes inclusion work. This is the real work of inclusive schools—the daily planning and instruction delivered through multiple adults, and when it happens well, it is like magic."

—Janice (principal)

"We've each been invited to this present moment by design. Our lives are joined together like the tiles of a mosaic; none of us contributes the whole of the picture, but each of us is necessary for its completion."

—Casey and Vanceburg (1996)

All students in a classroom community can benefit from a team of educators that includes teachers, therapists, and paraprofessionals working together in ways that promote meaningful learning and a sense of belonging for all students. In an inclusive school, the supporting adults are like tiles of a mosaic. Each person is an important contributor to the larger picture. In today's inclusive schools and classrooms, it is quite common for general education teachers and special education teachers to work alongside paraprofessionals and therapists to co-deliver instruction. Getting the multiple adults to work effectively together—creating effective instructional teams—is one of the most important roles in leading inclusive schools. This chapter provides information and tools that will enable leading effective collaboration. We begin by identifying ineffective practices or common pitfalls and then explain the principal's role as instructional leader as well as the other key roles of the instructional teams. We propose general ways to develop teams and provide effective communication, as well as concepts the principal will need to understand in order to help the team co-deliver instruction. Then, we discuss some of the ethical considerations of confidentiality inherent in inclusive schools. Finally, we address commonly asked questions about collaboration.

COMMON PITFALLS

To achieve effective collaboration, it is essential for the principal to maximize the human resources at his or her school in order to ensure all students' participation and learning. There are a number of common but ineffective practices we believe it is important for leaders to understand in order to help avoid them. First, it is common to see multiple adults in inclusive classrooms. Many times, these precious resources are used poorly. When observing classrooms, we often see the special education teacher playing only a glorified assistant's role; or we see teachers, therapists, and paraprofessionals sitting for significant blocks of time with little instructional role; or we see that one adult (often the general education teacher) is doing all of the instruction and the other adults are attached to one or two students with disabilities, providing overly intensive support. In scenarios like this, we see that special education teachers often feel devalued, paraprofessionals do not know their roles and are left to determine what is best for students with significant needs, and general education teachers are frustrated that the adults in the room are not more helpful. Effective collaboration seeks to maximize the use of all adults to provide effective inclusive services.

Another common issue is that, too often, teachers, therapists, and paraprofessionals work in isolation from each other. Whether in the general education classroom or in an overreliance on pulling students from the classroom, adults carry out their own plans, therapies, and instruction with no regard for or significant coordination with the rest of the student's day or program. This puts students in unfortunate situations where they feel the fragmentation of their day and education.

ROLES AND RESPONSIBILITIES

Roles and responsibilities of school staff vary among schools, districts, and even states. Nonetheless, despite these variations, there are generally accepted roles and responsibilities that hold true from school to school. This section provides some general guidelines for how school personnel can work effectively as a team to meet the needs of all students together. We begin with perhaps the most important role in a collaborative school: the principal's role.

The Principal's Role—Leading Collaboration

As you implement inclusive service delivery it is essential that you develop collaborative instructional teams. At the core of these teams are general educators and special educators who will work together most closely to meet the needs of the range of learners. This core needs special consideration in terms of matching the strengths of the teachers, giving them time to plan, and making sure they are a well-oiled team. The therapists, paraprofessionals, and other staff are also important. The principal, as leader, must play a number of key roles to foster collaboration.

First, you are responsible for creating these teams—putting specific special education teachers with specific general education teachers, assigning paraprofessionals to teams, and helping to create inclusive schedules for therapists and other specialists. We see that effective leaders in this regard both ask the teachers and staff to name colleagues with whom they believe they are best suited to collaborate, and also use their own knowledge of staff strengths and personalities to create teams. Once the teams are created, it is important to invest in developing the teams, both initially and in an ongoing manner. Later on in the chapter, we share some guiding questions to help team members come together, develop norms, and understand each other.

Second, you set and supervise the inclusive instructional expectations. This means explaining the expectations for teams in terms of co-planning and co-delivering of instruction: 1) that the instructional teams are expected to use common planning time to co-plan differentiated lessons and units with appropriate modifications, 2) that all adults who are in the classroom need meaningful roles during instruction, and 3) that a variety of co-teaching strategies need to be incorporated every day in the classroom. This also means that during walk-throughs and observations, you ascertain that instructional teams are co-delivering instruction to heterogeneous groups of students. You should celebrate the positive examples of co-planning and co-delivery of instruction and also confront situations in which teams might be grouping students with disabilities together and instructing them at the back table or when adults are not engaged in meaningful ways. We have created a tool for leaders to use to provide feedback to teams regarding collaboration and co-delivery of instruction; see Figure 5.1 for the co-delivery of instruction feedback form.

Third, your role is to provide time for planning. We recommend that teams have, at minimum, common planning time for 40–60 minutes, one to two times per week. Creating a master schedule in which instructional teams have sacred common planning time *must* be a leadership priority. We know that when teams do not plan together, their ability to collaborate and co-deliver instruction is significantly impaired, resulting in wasting precious human resources and providing much less effective services to students.

Fourth, your role is to provide teams with professional development on collaboration and co-teaching strategies. We know that the greatest challenges to inclusive schools and classrooms are the adults. One of the challenges comes from the fact that teachers often do not know—and have not had professional development on—how to work effectively with other teachers, paraprofessionals, and staff. We know that professional learning around collaboration can produce significant results in creating effective instructional teams. As with all professional development, this must be ongoing and built into the culture of the school, so that as new teams are created, this professional learning is part of the ethos of the school. See the Commonly Asked Questions section at the end of this chapter for ideas and resources. Providing professional development on the following skills is a key to effective change:

- Team development

- Running meetings—using agendas, minutes, and other meeting tools (a team meeting minutes form is provided in Figure 5.2)

- Co-planning

- Co-delivery of instruction and co-teaching strategies

- Role release

- Working with paraprofessionals

Instructional Team:
Co-Delivery of Instruction Feedback Form

	Date: Time:
Lesson/content:	Co-teachers: 1. 2.
	Other adults present:

Model:	Check one:	Describe the co-teaching model used:
One teach, one observe*		
Parallel teaching		
Station teaching		
Alternative teaching*		
Team teaching		
One teach, one assist*		

	Look for:	Evidence:	Descriptions:
Leadership in class	Both teachers take a lead role in the class.	❑ Not evident ❑ Emerging ❑ Evident ❑ Much evidence	What is each teacher's role?
	Students relate to both teachers as leaders.	❑ Not evident ❑ Emerging ❑ Evident ❑ Much evidence	What are students' attitudes regarding teachers?

*Use sparingly and on occasion only.

(continued)

Figure 5.1. Instructional Team: Co-Delivery of Instruction Feedback Form.

Figure 5.1.   *(continued)*

(page 2 of 3)

Accommodations and modifications	Both teachers provide appropriate accommodations and modifications for students with disabilities.	☐ Not evident ☐ Emerging ☐ Evident ☐ Much evidence	How do teachers accommodate and modify instruction?
	Students work at appropriately accommodated and modified tasks.	☐ Not evident ☐ Emerging ☐ Evident ☐ Much evidence	What specific accommodations and modifications are used by students?
Behavior management	Both teachers share behavior management and use positive behavior support strategies.	☐ Not evident ☐ Emerging ☐ Evident ☐ Much evidence	How does each teacher support students to behave appropriately?
	Students respond to either teacher's intervention with appropriate behavior.	☐ Not evident ☐ Emerging ☐ Evident ☐ Much evidence	Describe student responses.
Access to all students	Special educator and general educator work with all students.	☐ Not evident ☐ Emerging ☐ Evident ☐ Much evidence	How does each teacher work with all students?
	All students work with both teachers.	☐ Not evident ☐ Emerging ☐ Evident ☐ Much evidence	How do students work with both teachers?
Grouping	Teachers work mostly with heterogeneous groups, shifting homogeneous groups often, if used.	☐ Not evident ☐ Emerging ☐ Evident ☐ Much evidence	Describe flow of student groups.
	Student groups change often, and homogeneous grouping is used sparingly.	☐ Not evident ☐ Emerging ☐ Evident ☐ Much evidence	Describe student grouping.

(continued)

Figure 5.1. *(continued)*   *(page 3 of 3)*

Active learning structures and learning styles	Teachers use active learning structures and multiple learning styles throughout the lesson.	❑ Not evident ❑ Emerging ❑ Evident ❑ Much evidence	What active learning structures and styles are taught?
	Students are actively engaged with multiple learning styles.	❑ Not evident ❑ Emerging ❑ Evident ❑ Much evidence	Describe student activity.

Comments: _____

_____

_____

_____

_____

Team Meeting Minutes

Date: _____

Team members present and assigned roles: **Team members absent:**

Facilitator:

Recorder:

Timekeeper:

Consensus builder:

Observer:

Today's agenda items	I - Information D - Discussion R - Requires decision	Presenter	Time guidelines
1.			
2.			
3.			
4.			
5.			
6.			

Items discussed: (continued)

Figure 5.2.   Team Meeting Minutes form.

Figure 5.2. *(continued)* (page 2 of 2)

Task delegated, time lines, follow-up:

Activity	Person responsible	Time line

Agenda items for next meeting:

1.

2.

3.

4.

5.

6.

Next meeting date: _____

Fifth, your support takes both symbolic and material forms. The symbolic support involves treating all teachers on instructional teams as equals and full members of the teams. This can include such practices as having both names on class lists, classroom doors, and communication with families and other practices that send a symbolic message that this instructional team together serves this group of students. Material support takes the form of providing supplies and curriculum. This can mean allocating additional resources, as both the general education and special education teachers require teacher guides and necessary teaching supplies (e.g., manipulatives for mathematics). This also takes the form of making sure both teachers have similar space (e.g., a teacher's desk) to organize their work.

The Instructional Team

The following sections describe the various educators who should make up an instructional team. We recognize that not all of these people will be on every team, but these are the key players across the range of teams most schools have.

The Special Educator

By definition, a special educator has earned a college degree in teaching. A special educator is partly responsible for designing each student's IEP. Each year, a team of teachers and parents determines each student's goals and objectives and the appropriate special education services. The special education teacher helps to ensure that the goals and objectives on each student's IEP are met. In collaboration with general education teachers and support staff, the special education teacher is responsible for helping to differentiate curricula and instruction and provides and recommends modifications and adaptations that would be appropriate for each student. Certainly, this means attention to and significant regard to students with disabilities, but special educators in effective instructional teams use this expertise in adaptation and individualization to benefit all students—those with and without disabilities. Special education teachers are also responsible for solving problems that arise in the classroom, evaluating each student's services, and communicating student progress to the team.

In effective inclusive instructional teams, the special educator plays a lead role in planning and delivering content to all children in the classroom—from kindergarten through twelfth grade. Co-planned instruction should happen in both large and small groups, using a variety of co-teaching strategies. However, a key to inclusive classrooms is to use heterogeneous groupings; therefore, special educators should work not only with students with disabilities and it should not be common practice to see those students grouped together at the back table. Remember: having the special education teacher act as a glorified teaching assistant is not a productive use of resources or teacher abilities.

The General Educator

A general educator is the other key member of the instructional team and he or she should be expected to educate all of the students in his or her class—those with and without disabilities. A general educator typically plans lessons, teaches these lessons, and assesses each student's skill. Typically, a general educator is considered the content expert for the particular grade level being taught.

In effective inclusive instructional teams, general educators co-plan and co-deliver instruction with special educators. They share responsibility for content and delivery. They may have great content expertise, but they are also responsible for differentiating the content and instruction for all learners. General educators take both lead and supporting roles on their teams for large group, small group, and individualized instruction. It is appropriate to expect that general educators will have as much or more contact with and be as or more responsible for the education of students with disabilities.

The Paraprofessional   Paraprofessionals are expected to perform many different tasks. Their focus is on supporting students and supporting instruction.

Often, the paraprofessional works under the supervision of the building principal, but the daily work is directed by special and general educators. It is important to recognize that both special and general educators need to see their role as planning for and communicating with paraprofessionals. Effective use of paraprofessionals means that the paraprofessionals provide nonintrusive support to all students in classrooms—not only to students with disabilities. The paraprofessional reviews and reinforces instruction to pre-K–12 students with a variety of disabilities in inclusive school, community, and vocational settings.

It is essential that the paraprofessional *not* be seen as the expert on a particular student and therefore not be relied upon to plan and take charge of that student's education. Too often, we see that the education of students with significant needs is left in the hands of or delegated to paraprofessionals—with teachers abdicating responsibility for these students. Paraprofessionals are key members of instructional teams and should be valued, but they should play a supporting role under the direction of certified general and special education teachers. Some essential functions of paraprofessionals include working with students with significant needs on daily living tasks, maintaining records, and providing instructional, emotional, and behavioral support for students with and without disabilities under a teacher's direction.

The Family   Family members are undoubtedly the most important people in a child's life. With the reauthorization of IDEA 2004 (PL 108-446), parents or guardians became equal members of students' IEP teams. Parents or guardians are expected to be active members of their children's education teams, because they know their children in ways that no one else does. Leaders, teachers, and paraprofessionals can help parents play active roles by communicating all that happens in the school setting and, further, by listening closely to the wishes and concerns of family members. Effective instructional teams involve families and communicate actively with them.

Occupational Therapists   For a student who works with an OT, the student's disability necessitates support in daily life skills. The therapist may evaluate the student's needs, provide therapy, modify classroom equipment, and generally help the student participate as fully as possible in school programs and activities. A therapist may work with children individually or lead small groups. Therapists also may consult with teachers and paraprofessionals to help students meet their goals within the context of general education settings. Specific types of therapies may include help with handwriting, computer work, fostering social play, teaching life skills such as getting dressed or eating with utensils. The difference between the role of OT and PT can be confusing; in general, OTs work more with fine motor skills and PTs work more with gross motor skills. It is important to embed these skills naturally within the general education classroom and daily schedule.

Physical Therapists

Physical therapy, like occupational therapy, is a related service and is provided by a qualified and licensed PT. PTs address areas such as gross motor development skills, orthopedic concerns, mobility, adaptive equipment, positioning needs, and other functional skills that may interfere with students' educational performance. Similar to an OT, a PT either works with individual students or leads small groups. PTs also consult with teachers and paraprofessionals. Specific types of therapies include practice walking up and down stairs safely, stretching after sustained sitting in a wheelchair, or help performing other physical activities. Again, these services are most effective when embedded into the natural flow of general education. This requires collaboration and a flexible mindset to see beyond traditional pullout therapy.

Speech and Language Therapists

Speech and language therapists (sometimes called speech-language pathologists, or SLPs) help students with communication and with all of the skills required to communicate effectively. These skills include all issues related to language, the voice, swallowing, and fluency. Some students who work with SLPs have issues with stuttering. Others work on understanding and producing language. In schools, SLPs collaborate with teaching teams to support classroom activities and effective communication. These services can also be seamlessly integrated into general education—but that does not happen without making it a priority and creating opportunities to collaborate.

IMPORTANT NOTE: Too often, well-intentioned but misguided schools do not try to bring occupational therapy, physical therapy, and speech-language therapy into the general education setting. These services are often the "last holdout" for inclusion. Effective inclusive teams make it a priority for all services to be delivered in an inclusive setting and create planning time with key players to make it happen. Effective inclusive schools do not leave occupational therapy, physical therapy, and speech-language therapy as separate pullout services but find ways to integrate planning and delivery into general education.

Psychologists The goals of school psychologists are to help children and youth succeed academically, socially, and emotionally. School psychologists work closely with teaching teams to create healthy and safe learning environments and to strengthen connections between each student's home and school. Psychologists assess students and are often involved in standardized testing to determine whether a student qualifies as having a disability. Psychologists also work directly with others on teaching teams by helping to problem-solve and, at times, provide direct support services to students.

Social Workers Like psychologists, school social workers help provide links connecting each student's home, school, and community. The services provided by social workers are intended to help enable students and families to overcome problems that may impede learning. School social workers provide individual and group counseling, consult with teachers, and teach or encourage social skills. They collaborate with community agencies and provide service coordination for students who require many different agencies or services.

Vision Teachers and Audiologists Vision teachers support students who have visual impairments or blindness. Vision teachers typically work with classroom teachers to make modifications and adaptations to the curricula. They also help provide needed equipment (e.g., magnifiers, computer equipment). Audiologists typically work with students who have hearing impairments, providing amplification systems and sign language interpreters for students who are deaf. A key role of these professionals is to help make the general education room and day most meaningful and successful for students with specific needs. Clearly, a vision specialist who removes a child from the class two times per week for 30 minutes at a time for vision support will have a less powerful impact on the education of that student than if he or she collaborated with the instructional team to enhance and make accessible the entire school day.

HOW DO ALL THESE PEOPLE WORK TOGETHER?

Every school differs, but one thing is certain: all the adults on a teaching team must work together for the purpose of promoting student growth. One example of effective collaboration involves a seventh-grade team.

· · · · · · ·

This team involves all of the staff who support Sara, a student with autism who struggles with reading. The core team of people supporting Sara in English class includes the English teacher, the special education teacher, and a paraprofessional. This team meets monthly to discuss Sara's support in English class. Every week, the special education teacher and the English teacher meet with the paraprofessional to create materials for upcoming units of study. In addition, the special education teacher and the English teacher plan lessons together with Sara in mind so that each lesson is designed to meet Sara's needs. For example, they planned a unit using a book from The Hunger Games *series. The teachers decided to have the entire class listen to an audio version of the book instead of reading silently. The paraprofessional receives written plans each day. This plan outlines the anticipated type and level of support that Sara needs during each activity.*

• • • • • • •

GUIDING QUESTIONS FOR INSTRUCTIONAL TEAMS

We find that it is important for instructional teams to get to know each other on a personal and professional level. This is necessary for real and effective collaboration to occur. Some questions that will help instructional team members learn about one another are listed in this section. The list can be approached as some simple suggestions, or teams may go through each question. We have seen many recently formed teams use these questions to build a foundation for their upcoming collaboration. We have also seen teams discuss one question each time they plan as a way to embed this team building on an ongoing but efficient basis. Clearly, there are many more questions that teams can use, but we have found these to be a good beginning.

Work Styles

- Are you a morning or afternoon person?
- How direct are you?
- Do you like to do several things at once, or do you prefer doing one thing at a time?
- How do you prefer to give feedback to others on the team?
- What do you consider your strengths and weaknesses when working in a team situation?

Philosophy

- To me, advanced planning means . . .
- All kids learn best when . . .
- In general, I think the best way to deal with challenging behavior is . . .
- In general, I think it is important to increase student independence by . . .
- I think our team relationship needs to be . . .

Logistics

- How should we communicate about students' history and progress?
- How should we communicate about our roles and responsibilities?
- How and when should we communicate about lessons and modifications?

- If I do not know an answer in class, should I direct the student to you?

- Do we meet often enough? If not, when should we meet?

- How do we communicate with the families? What is each person's role in this?

- Are there other logistical concerns?

Questions for the Family

- How would you like to communicate about your child's progress?

- If we are using a communication notebook or e-mail, how often would you like to hear from the school?

- Are there things you are especially interested in hearing about?

After having personal discussions using these questions as a guide, teams are better able to negotiate the logistical and philosophical components of teamwork, allowing team members to feel more comfortable in knowing the roles and expectations within the classroom setting. The next section describes common co-teaching arrangements that should give further clarity to the collaborative work of adults in the classroom.

CO-TEACHING ARRANGEMENTS

In this section, we describe common co-teaching arrangements from Friend and Reising (1993) and Friend and Bursuck (2011). It is important to note that these strategies can and should be used whenever there are multiple adults in a classroom. A common and misguided conception is that only when a classroom has two teachers for the entire day or for an entire period or block can teams use these strategies. That is simply not true. Instructional teams need to plan meaningful roles for all adults, and we recommend using the following co-teaching arrangements to guide that planning. This gives teams a common language and a common framework to talk about and plan for utilizing multiple adults.

You can and should expect that any time two or more educators share the instructional responsibility for a group of students within a single classroom setting, they utilize a variety of co-teaching arrangements. Educators can include a general education teacher, a special education teacher, therapists or other specialists, and paraprofessionals who work together to deliver special education services for students with disabilities within the general education context. In the following subsections, we share six common arrangements.

Parallel Teaching

A heterogeneous class is split into two groups, providing a smaller teacher-to-student ratio. Teachers have the same objectives and divide the class and teach simultaneously.

The process of learning could also be different. If one teacher is particularly skilled at visual-spatial content delivery, that lesson utilizes pictures, while the other teacher emphasizes learning through hands-on learning experiences. This approach might be used for teaching nonfiction text features using two different science topics (e.g., electricity and life cycles).

Station Teaching

A heterogeneous class is split into three groups. Teachers co-plan the stations. Two stations are educator-facilitated, while one station allows students to work independently, in pairs, or as a cooperative group. Students rotate to each of the stations, while each educator is the lead instructor at one station. Each teacher teaches the content to one group, then repeats the instruction for the other groups.

Team Teaching

Educators share leadership in the instruction and classroom activities. One teacher might read a story aloud while the other teacher creates a corresponding concept map. One teacher might lead a social studies lesson, while the other teacher might demonstrate note-taking skills. Both teachers have an interdependent role with the large group instruction.

One Teach, One Observe

One teacher leads the lesson while the other gathers data on students. For example, while one teacher leads a geography lesson, the other teacher records observations in the form of anecdotal notes and uses a checklist on students' learning and misconceptions. Teachers might collect data on student's participation during group discussions, independent work, decoding skills, and more. It is imperative that teachers rotate these roles so each is able to lead instruction and observe class learning experiences.

Alternative Teaching

One teacher works with most of the class while the other provides instruction for a small group. This small group could be used for preteaching core concepts in order to provide background knowledge for the upcoming lesson or unit. It could also be used to provide enrichment experiences for students who have mastered the grade-level content objectives. This approach should be used cautiously so it does not become a remediation group in the back of the classroom. This option must be used along with the other co-teaching options and only used occasionally.

One Teach, One Assist

One teacher leads the lesson while the other provides unobtrusive assistance to individual students. This assisting teacher may answer questions, keep students on task, and provide prompt support to students who need it. Educators must switch roles and both take the lead of instruction so that one adult is not always merely assisting. Again, this option should be used sparingly and along with other co-teaching options.

> **IMPORTANT NOTE:** Researchers have found the arrangement one teach, one assist to be the most commonly used and the least effective. Thus, it is imperative that leaders make clear that they expect teams not to rely on this strategy.

In addition to these co-teaching strategies, Table 5.1 and Figure 5.3 provide concrete ideas for helping staff think about roles in common classroom situations.

Table 5.1. Ideas for roles for multiple adults in the classroom

If one teacher is doing this	Another teacher can be doing this
Lecturing	Modeling notetaking on the board, drawing the ideas on the board, or taking notes on the overhead
Taking attendance	Collecting and reviewing homework
Giving directions	Writing the directions on the board so all students have a place to look for the visual cues
Providing large-group instruction	Collecting data on student behavior or engagement, or making modifications for an upcoming lesson
Giving a test	Reading the test to students who prefer to have the test read to them
Facilitating stations or small groups	Also facilitating stations or groups
Facilitating sustained, silent reading	Reading aloud quietly with a small group
Teaching a new concept	Providing visuals or models to enhance the whole group's understanding
Reteaching or preteaching with a small group	Monitoring the large group as students work independently

Source: Murawski and Dieker (2004).

Determining Roles and Responsibilities Among Team Members

....

Directions: Read through the following common roles and responsibilities. Determine which team member should take on each of the roles and responsibilities:

P = Primary responsibility   S = Secondary responsibility

Sh = Shared responsibility   I = Input in the decision making

Major role or responsibility	Classroom teacher	Special education teacher	Paraprofessional	Other
Developing student objectives				
Designing differentiated curriculum				
Creating student-specific modifications and adaptations				
Creating classroom materials				
Co-teaching curriculum				
Providing one-to-one instruction				
Teaching the whole class of students				
Leading small groups				
Monitoring student progress				
Examining student work to determine next steps				
Assessing and assigning grades				
Communicating with parents				
Consulting with related service personnel				
Participating in IEP meetings				

Figure 5.3. Determining Roles and Responsibilities Among Team Members form.

(continued)

From Causton-Theoharis, J. (2003). *Increasing interactions between students with disabilities and their peers via paraprofessional training* (Unpublished doctoral dissertation). University of Wisconsin–Madison; adapted by permission.

In *The Principal's Handbook for Leading Inclusive Schools* by Julie Causton and George Theoharis
(2014, Paul H. Brookes Publishing Co., Inc.)

Figure 5.3. *(continued)* (page 2 of 2)

Disciplining students				
Writing in communication notebooks				
Providing community-based programming				

Major role or responsibility	Classroom teacher	Special education teacher	Therapist	Paraprofessional
Developing peer supports				
Scheduling common planning time				
Participating in regularly scheduled team planning meetings				
Facilitating meetings				
Communicating information from meetings to other team members				
Other				

When you have finished determining roles and responsibilities for each of the team members, ask yourselves the following questions:

1. Could any of these roles and responsibilities be shared or changed?

2. Does anyone feel uncomfortable with any of the roles as outlined?

3. Does anyone believe he or she needs more information or training to perform the above-mentioned responsibilities?

4. What messages are sent to students, parents, and others about the way adults work together as a team in this classroom through the division of responsibilities?

5. What changes need to be made?

From Causton-Theoharis, J. (2003). *Increasing interactions between students with disabilities and their peers via paraprofessional training* (Unpublished doctoral dissertation). University of Wisconsin–Madison; adapted by permission.

In *The Principal's Handbook for Leading Inclusive Schools* by Julie Causton and George Theoharis
(2014, Paul H. Brookes Publishing Co., Inc.)

WHAT IF CONFLICT ARISES?

"The kids aren't the hard part of my job. It is working with other adults that I find challenging."

—Pam (paraprofessional)

Ideal team functioning is like a well-oiled machine in which each cog runs continually and smoothly, each harmoniously performing an individual function for the good of the entire machine. However, in reality, team functioning does not always go this smoothly. Conflicts among adults do arise.

We know that school leaders have a host of skills in resolving conflict. We provide one method here as an important acknowledgment that the need for conflict resolution is a reality when adults work together. The Bonner Foundation, a nonprofit education organization, has suggested eight steps for conflict resolution. Conflict is defined as "a mental or physical disagreement in which people's values or needs are in opposition to each other or they think that they are opposed" (Bonner Foundation, 2008). The Bonner Foundation's suggestions for handling conflicts are listed here, along with our related suggestions:

1. "Identify positions ('what are they saying') of each side of the people in conflict." Write down your perspective and the other person's perspective.

2. "Learn more about true needs and desires behind each side." Write down your beliefs about the other person's needs and desires. Write down your own needs and desires.

3. "Ask clarifying questions for more information." Ask the other person, "Why do you feel the way you do?" "What do you think you need in this situation?" Reframe the problem into a question.

4. "Brainstorm possible solutions." Without judging the ideas, write down as many ideas as you can.

5. "Discuss how each solution would affect each side, and figure out possible compromises." Talk through each of the potential solutions. Discuss which ones would work and which ones would not work, from your perspective and from the other person's perspective. Generate more ideas, if necessary.

6. "Agree on a solution." Determine which solution would work the best for both of you. Write out a plan for carrying out the solution and determine how long you plan to implement the solution.

7. "Implement solutions." Give your idea a try for the determined amount of time.

8. "Reevaluate solutions, if necessary." Come back together to discuss the solution and what is working or not working about this solution. Continue the process as necessary.

MAKING THE TIME TO COMMUNICATE

We have spoken with hundreds of instructional teams across the country, and one of the most common problems they mention involves not having enough time to communicate or collaborate. Different teams have solved this problem by using several different strategies. We describe those strategies in the following list. This can be a resource for principals and teams to find ways to help improve communication. The following strategies have been successfully used to carve out more meeting time:

1. *Video or independent work time*—Create a weekly meeting time during which students are expected to watch instructional videos or to work independently for 15 minutes. Allow them to watch or work independently while the team meets.

2. *Use a parent volunteer*—As a parent volunteer reads a book to the students or leads a review game, meet together for 15 minutes.

3. *Use another teacher team*—Put two classrooms together for a half-hour each week for a certain portion of the curriculum or community-building activities. One teaching team supervises the students while the other team meets. The teams then switch.

4. *Meet during specials time*—Ask the specials teachers whether their classes have any 15-minute periods that might not require paraprofessional support. Specifically use that time to meet and communicate with paraprofessionals.

5. *Meet before or after school*—Take 15 minutes before or after school to have a "sacred" meeting time for teaching teams.

If you simply cannot use any of these strategies to elicit more face-to-face meeting times, some teams have come up with alternatives to meeting face to face:

1. *Communication notebook*—Establish a notebook that all members of the team read and respond to each day. Team members can write questions in the notebook and obtain responses. Notebooks also can be used to discuss schedules or student-specific information.

2. *E-mail*—E-mail can be substituted for the communication notebook; team members can contact each other with questions, comments, or schedule changes.

3. *Mailbox*—Use a mailbox in the classroom for each staff member. Direct all notes or general information to that place.

4. *Electronic/cloud sharing*—Use a file sharing web site (e.g., Google Docs, Dropbox) as a shared space for plans, notes, and communication.

5. *Proofread*—As notes are written that go home to the students' parents, have the teaching team proofread each of the notes. This way, not only are the notes proofread, but everyone receives all of the necessary information.

6. *Lesson plan sharing*—Keep lesson plans out and accessible to all members of the team. Use the notes to communicate about upcoming content. Ask the person who writes the plans to delineate each team member's role for each lesson.

ETHICAL CONSIDERATIONS: CONFIDENTIALITY

Confidentiality is an important issue and plays a different role in inclusive schools. As instructional teams assume shared responsibility for the range of students, it is essential that students' needs and struggles stay private and not become fodder for school or community gossip. All members of instructional teams will have to be careful when others ask questions about school situations. Many parents and community members might ask for details about student behavior, disability, or activities. Teams can think of ways to deflect potentially inappropriate personal questions that require maintaining confidentiality. For example, a parent approaches a teacher or paraprofessional and says, "I notice you work with Lucy. Why does she need a walker?" Teams can consider being ready to say something such as, "I am sorry, but school confidentiality does not allow me to talk about that. It is not okay for me to talk about another child with you." Then, the teacher can direct the parent to someone with whom he or she can talk: "Feel free to ask [the principal]."

COMMONLY ASKED QUESTIONS ABOUT COLLABORATION

Q. What are some good resources for collaboration or co-teaching strategies?

A. Barger-Anderson, R., Isherwood, R.S., & Merhaut, J. (2013). *Strategic co-teaching in your school: Using the co-design model.* Baltimore, MD: Paul H. Brookes Publishing Co.; Friend, M. (2005). *The Power of 2* [DVD]. Available from www.forumoneducation.org; Friend, M., & Cook, L. (2006). *Interactions: Collaboration skills for school professionals* (4th ed.). Boston, MA: Allyn & Bacon; Snell, M., & Janney, R. (2005). *Teachers' guides to inclusive practices: Collaborative teaming* (2nd ed.). Baltimore, MD: Paul H. Brookes Publishing Co.; Villa, R., Thousand, J., & Nevin, A. (2008). *A guide to co-teaching: A multimedia kit for professional development* [multimedia]. Thousand Oaks, CA: Corwin Press.

Q. Our instructional teams are working pretty well, but paraprofessionals say, "I am not sure what I am supposed to be doing in art class [or other special-area classes]. We [the art teacher and I] have never talked, so mostly I just sit and support two students. What should I do?"

A. Set up a time for the paraprofessional to meet with the art teacher so they come to a shared understanding about how the paraprofessional can be most useful to the students in this class, how he or she can best support the teacher, and what the teacher would like the paraprofessional to do or not do. These kinds of communication are crucial in any classroom where multiple adults are providing support.

Q. I have read about co-teaching arrangements, but I do not see any of them in my school. What can I do?

A. Provide your instructional teams with information and learning about these arrangements—using this book and other resources listed. Begin a conversation with each team, asking how they will use the arrangements in their planning for the coming week. While doing observations and walk-throughs, check to see that the arrangements being used reinforce your expectations that teams use multiple co-teaching strategies. Feel free to use the feedback tool provided in Figure 5.1.

Q. Some of my teachers are not comfortable playing new roles in classrooms. What do I do about that?

A. Communicate your expectations about teams sharing responsibility for all students. Reinforce that new roles are an essential part of this shared responsibility and that feelings of discomfort are a natural part of this process. Remember that change is hard for people and that even well-intentioned professionals need nudging to engage in new ways of doing their work.

CONCLUSION

The principal's role in creating and leading inclusive instructional teams is one of the most crucial aspects of this work. It requires a lot of attention and planning. Teams require support in many ways. The principal will have to disband teams each year and create new ones, so the professional learning about collaboration and co-teaching arrangements needs to become an ongoing part of the school community.

We know that working with multiple adults on a team can be challenging but, like Principal Janice said at the beginning of this chapter, when the team comes together it can be magical and have a remarkably positive impact on the learning of students. Remember that effective instructional teams are developed purposefully and co-plan and co-deliver instruction. This requires having common planning time and using it effectively, using the variety of co-teaching arrangements for the multiple adults, and establishing effective communication. The magic of inclusive collaboration is much more likely to happen when the principal as a leader makes it a priority and plays this key role.

NOTES

_____

_____

_____

_____

_____

_____

_____

_____

_____

_____

_____

_____

_____

_____

_____

_____

_____

_____

_____

_____

_____

_____

_____

_____

_____

_____

_____

_____

6

Rethinking Students

Presuming Competence

THE MOST APPROPRIATE LABEL IS
USUALLY THE ONE PEOPLE'S PARENTS
HAVE GIVEN THEM.

"I used to walk past those rooms and see kids working on puzzles and swinging on the big swings. I thought, 'That's nice, those students are really working at their level.' But then, we got a new special education teacher and she expected students to be included. I just watched Jacob, the very same student who used to spend his days swinging and doing puzzles, do a PowerPoint presentation in his civics class. He was the same student who had been working on writing his name and address last year. I realized we greatly underestimated what these students can accomplish!"

—Ben (principal)

"When I approach a child, [s]he inspires in me two sentiments: tenderness for what [s]he is, and respect for what [s]he may become."

—Louis Pasteur (Institut Pasteur, n.d.)

This chapter introduces the concept of *rethinking students*. Rethinking a student entails getting to know about the student and then reflecting on how you see, treat, and work with him or her. First, we discuss how to describe students to others through student strengths and multiple intelligences. Then, we describe the concept of presumption of competence and using age-appropriate and person-first language.

STUDENT DESCRIPTIONS

Shawntell Strully is a 22-year-old who lives in her own home with roommates, attends classes at Colorado State University, volunteers on campus, travels during spring break, gets around in her own car, has her own interests, likes and desires, has a boyfriend, and speaks out on issues of concern to her.

Shawntell Strully is 22 years old, is severely/profoundly mentally retarded, is hearing impaired, visually impaired, has cerebral palsy, has a seizure disorder, does not chew her food (and sometimes chokes), is not toilet trained, has no verbal communication, has no reliable communication system, and has a developmental age of 17–24 months. (Strully & Strully, 1996, pp. 144–145)

These two radically different descriptions of Shawntell come from two different groups of people. The first description comes from her parents. The second comes from her teachers and other school support personnel. Although not all teachers would describe Shawntell in these ways, this is how her team described her. It is surprising to compare these statements side-by-side. The stark contrast raises the question of how the same person can be described in such disparate ways.

The principal reason for these radically different descriptions is that each group of people looks for different things and approaches Shawntell from a different perspective. Shawntell's parents know her deeply. They have spent a great deal of time with her, know her intimately, and understand her as a person who has wide interests and capabilities. Their description of her cites her interests, gifts, and talents. Conversely, the description generated by Shawntell's teachers reflects a more distant understanding of her; it is a cold, clinical account that focuses exclusively on her impairments.

School principals will hear impairment-driven descriptions of students and, thus, will need to work to understand these students through their strengths, gifts, and talents. A principal may read a student's individualized education program and it might abound with phrases such as *mental age of 2, phobic,* or *aggressive.* Reading those descriptors, the principal will need to realize that he or she is getting only one perspective on the student. It is important to get to know the student and work to learn about what he or she can do. Staff should be encouraged to look for the student's gifts, strengths, and talents. The goal is for a team's descriptions of a student to look much closer to the parents' perspective on Shawntell than that of the teachers.

BEGIN WITH STRENGTHS

Susan, a principal, described Daniel, a student in her school, as autistic, limited, busy, energetic, having a good sense of humor, and detail oriented. These descriptions speak to Susan's own beliefs about the student. On a piece of paper, write down the first 10 descriptors that come to mind when you think of an individual student. Now, look over the list. Were your descriptors positive, negative, or a combination?

The school staff's beliefs about a student will affect how they support and work with that student. For example, if they believe a student is lazy or defiant, they will approach him or her in a different way than if they believe that child is motivated or cooperative. Your staff can alter their beliefs about students by spending some time rethinking them. Reframing your conceptions of students in more positive ways creates opportunities for growth.

Consider the work of educational researcher Thomas Armstrong (2000a, 2000b) on using multiple intelligences theory in the classroom. Armstrong recommended that education professionals purposefully rethink the ways they describe students. By changing their language, people will begin to change their impressions. Armstrong emphasized that all behavior is part of the human experience and that behavior is based on a multitude of influences (e.g., environment, sense of safety, personal well-being). Armstrong has proposed that, instead of considering a child *learning disabled,* people should see the child as *learning differently.* Table 6.1 lists further suggestions for describing students.

What would happen if all education professionals changed how they viewed and spoke about students? What if every student were viewed as a capable learner? One of the best ways to think about the students you oversee is to look at the child through the lens of his or her strengths. Ask yourself the following questions: "What can this student do?" "What are this person's strengths?" "How would a parent who deeply loves this student speak about him or her?" Now, return to your list and take a moment to develop a list of strengths, gifts, and interests.

During a workshop with a group of teachers and paraprofessionals, Kathy, a paraprofessional, did just that. First, she wrote a list of descriptors. Then, after spending some time rethinking the student, she came up with a completely different list.

Table 6.1. Turning lead into gold

A child who is judged to be	Can also be considered
Learning disabled	Learning differently
Hyperactive	Kinesthetic
Impulsive	Spontaneous
ADD/ADHD[a]	A bodily kinesthetic learner
Dyslexic	A spatial learner
Aggressive	Assertive
Plodding	Thorough
Lazy	Relaxed
Immature	Late blooming
Phobic	Cautious
Scattered	Divergent
Daydreaming	Imaginative
Irritable	Sensitive
Perseverative	Persistent

From Armstrong, T. (2000a). "Table 10-1: Turning lead into gold", from IN THEIR OWN WAY by Thomas Armstrong, copyright © 1987, 2000 by Thomas Armstrong. Used by permission of Jeremy P. Tarcher, an imprint of Penguin Group (USA) LLC.

[a]ADD, attention deficit disorder; ADHD, attention-deficit/hyperactivity disorder.

She had originally described the student, Brian, as "lazy, smart, sneaky, a liar, cute, cunning, and mean (at times)." After talking about viewing students differently, she got a new piece of paper. She wrote, "relaxed, intelligent, good in math, cute, needs some support with peer relationships, a great sense of humor, and a beautiful smile." We asked Kathy whether this still accurately described Brian. She said that the second list was a much more accurate description of him.

MULTIPLE INTELLIGENCES

There is a pervasive myth in education that some people are smart and others are not. *Intelligence, academic potential,* and *competence* are words often used to describe "smartness." In education, this belief can be seen best through the system of labeling people with disabilities. A clear example is IQ testing. Students take IQ tests, and if a student's IQ score falls below 70 and he or she has other issues with functional skills, the student receives the label of ID. Howard Gardner (1993) challenged the way psychologists and educators defined *intelligence* and offered a different way to look at intelligence. He used the term *multiple intelligences.*

Gardner viewed each of the multiple intelligences as a capacity that is inherent in the human brain and that is developed and expressed in social and cultural contexts.

Table 6.2. A guide to supporting through multiple intelligences

Intelligence	Which means	So support using
Verbal/linguistic intelligence	Good with words and language, written and spoken	Jokes, speeches, readings, stories, essays, the Internet, books, biographies
Logical mathematical intelligence	Preference for reasoning, numbers, and patterns	Mazes, puzzles, time lines, analogies, formulas, calculations, codes, games, probabilities
Spatial intelligence	Ability to visualize an object or to create mental images or pictures	Mosaics, drawings, illustrations, models, maps, videos, posters
Bodily kinesthetic intelligence	Knowledge or wisdom of the body and movement	Role-playing, skits, facial expressions, experiments, field trips, sports, games
Musical intelligence	Ability to recognize tonal patterns, including sensitivity to rhythms or beats	Performances, songs, instruments, rhythms, compositions, melodies, raps, jingles, choral readings
Interpersonal intelligence	Good with person-to-person interactions and relationships	Group projects, group tasks, observation dialogs, conversation, debate, games, interviews
Intrapersonal intelligence	Knowledge of an inner state of being; reflective and aware	Journals, meditation, self-assessment, recording, creative expression, goal setting, affirmation, poetry
Naturalistic intelligence	Knowledge of the outside world (e.g., plants, animals, weather patterns)	Field trips, observation, nature walks, forecasting, stargazing, fishing, exploring, categorizing, collecting, identifying

Sources: Armstrong (2000a, 2000b); Gardner (1993).

Instead of viewing intelligence as a fixed number on an aptitude test, Gardner argued that every person, regardless of disability label, is smart in different ways. All of the eight intelligences are described in Table 6.2. The column entitled "So support using" might help you think of ways to structure learning for the students you support. A teacher working with a student who prefers to learn in a certain intelligence area or who is strong in a certain area should consider some of the suggested activities and teaching styles. This is a great reference for a school's entire staff.

PRESUME COMPETENCE

In the school setting, assumptions about students can affect their education. Take Sue Rubin, for instance.

· · · · · · ·

Sue, a student with autism, had no formal way of communicating until she was 13 years old. Before that time, she had been treated and educated as if she had a mental age of 2 years old. Mental age is often based on a person's score on an IQ test. For example, if a 14-year-old girl's score on an IQ test was the score of a "typical" or "normal" 3-year-old, she would be labeled as having the mental age of a 3-year-old. This is not a useful way to think about intelligence. When Sue acquired a form of communication called facilitated communication, those long-held assumptions were no longer valid. People began to realize that she was very smart. She subsequently took advanced placement classes all through her high school career, and she is now in college (Biklen, 2005; Rubin, 2003).

· · · · · · ·

Because education professionals have no real way of determining what a student understands, they should presume that every student is competent or capable. Anne Donnellan used the term *least dangerous assumption* to describe this idea: "Least dangerous assumption states that in the absence of absolute evidence, it is essential to make the assumption that, if proven to be false, would be least dangerous to the individual" (1984, p. 24). In other words, it is better to presume that students are competent and that they can learn than to expect that they cannot learn.

Biklen and Burke (2006) have described this idea of presuming competence by explaining that outside observers (e.g., teachers, parents, paraprofessionals) have a choice: They can determine either that a person is competent or incompetent. The presumption of competence recognizes that no one can definitively know another person's thinking unless the other person can (accurately) reveal it. As Biklen and Burke put it, "Presuming competence refuses to limit opportunity . . . it casts the teachers, parents, and others in the role of finding ways to support the person to demonstrate his or her agency" (p. 167).

AGE-APPROPRIATE LANGUAGE

There is a tendency for people to speak down to individuals with disabilities (as if they were younger than they actually are) because of an assumption that people with disabilities are at younger developmental levels. For example, we have heard a paraprofessional ask a high school student, "Do you have to use the potty?" You would not ask a high school student who did not have a disability that same question in that same way. We also have overheard someone describe a young man with Down syndrome who attends college as "a real cutie." Individuals with disabilities should be described in accordance with their actual chronological ages.

All educators should treat and work with students in age-appropriate ways. It is important to be sure that your entire school staff understand age-appropriate treatment. We witnessed a paraprofessional holding hands with a sixth-grade student in the hall. We doubt that the paraprofessional would have thought it appropriate to hold the hand of a sixth-grade student who did not have a disability. For that very reason, it is inappropriate to hold any sixth-grade student's hand. This same logic holds true for having students sit on your lap, play with age-inappropriate toys, sing age-inappropriate songs, and so forth. Ask yourself how you would talk to or work with the student if she or he did not have a disability, and proceed in that manner.

PERSON-FIRST LANGUAGE

"If thoughts corrupt language, language can also corrupt thought."

—George Orwell (1946)

When describing, speaking, or writing respectfully about people who have disabilities, many people use a common language. It is called *person-first language*. The concept of person-first language is simple and is detailed in the following subsections.

The Same as Anyone Else

Think first about how you might introduce someone who does not have a disability. You might use the person's name, say how you know him or her, or describe what he or she does. The same is true for individuals with disabilities. Instead of saying, "Chelsea, who has Down syndrome," you might say, "Chelsea, who is in my fourth-grade class."

Table 6.3. Examples of person-first language

Say	Instead of	Because
People with disabilities	The disabled or handicapped	Place emphasis on the person.
People without disabilities	Normal/healthy/typical	The nonpreferred words assume the opposite for students with disabilities (e.g., abnormal, unhealthy, atypical).
Ella, the fourth-grade student	Ella, the student with Down syndrome	Omit the label whenever possible; it is most often not relevant.
Communicates with her eyes/device, and so forth	Is nonverbal	Focus on strengths.
Uses a wheelchair	Is confined to a wheelchair	Use possessive language to refer to assistive technologies; the nonpreferred language implies the person is "stuck."
Accessible parking spot	Handicapped parking spot	Use accurate representation.
Beth has autism.	Beth is autistic.	Emphasize that disability is one attribute—not a defining characteristic.
Gail has a learning disability.	Gail is learning disabled.	Emphasize that disability is one attribute—not a defining characteristic.
Jeff has a cognitive disability.	Jeff is retarded.	Emphasize that disability is one attribute—not a defining characteristic; also, *cognitive disability* is a preferred term.
Ben receives special education services.	Ben is in special education.	Special education is a service, not a place.
The student who is blind	The blind student	Place the person before the disability.
Denis writes using the computer.	Denis can't write with a pencil.	Focus on strengths.
Needs a magnifier, laptop, or cane	Problems with vision; can't write or walk	Focus on needs, not problems.

Source: Snow (2008).

No one should be identified by one aspect of who he or she is (especially if that aspect represents a difficulty or struggle for someone). For example, an author named Julie would not want anyone to introduce her by saying, "This is Julie, who struggles with statistics." The same is true when talking about a person with a disability. Ask yourself why you would need to mention that the person has a disability.

Words are powerful. The ways we talk about and describe people with disabilities do not just affect our beliefs and interactions with our students; they also provide models for others who hear these descriptions. If your own child broke his arm, would you introduce him or her to someone new as "my broken-armed child"? If one of the students in the school had cancer, would you expect to hear a teacher state, "She is my cancerous student"? Of course not. No one should feel ashamed about having a broken arm or having cancer, but a broken bone or malfunctioning cells do not define a person.

Avoid the Label

Would you like to be known for your medical history? Probably not. The same is true for people with disabilities. Yet, students with disabilities are invariably described with labels instead of person-first language. Have you ever heard phrases such as *the learning-disabled student, the autistic boy, that Downs child, the resource room kids,* or *the inclusion kids?*

It is important to understand the preferences of people with disabilities regarding how they would like others to speak about them. The guidelines listed in Table 6.3 come from two self-advocacy groups (www.disabilityisnatural.com and TASH).

COMMONLY ASKED QUESTIONS ABOUT RETHINKING STUDENTS

Q. How do I teach my staff about presumption of competence or age-appropriate language?

A. These are great topics for professional development. You can use this book as a starting place, or show videos of individuals who have disabilities to begin a discussion of presumption of competence. Excellent films include *Autism Is a World, Wretches and Jabberers,* and *Including Samuel.*

Q. What if a student prefers an age-inappropriate toy or game?

A. Often, people with disabilities have been treated as if they were younger than they are. As a result, they have been exposed to cartoons, dolls, or games that are inappropriate for their age, and their peers are not likely to think these activities are cool. One option, then, is to find out if a particular show or character is featured in more age-appropriate books, music, or activities.

Q. Are there any exceptions to person-first language?

A. Yes, people who are deaf often prefer the term *deaf* instead of *person with deafness*. A group called Deaf First suggests that deafness is a major component of identity, and this group prefers disability-first language. Some people with autism prefer to be called *autistic,* and some use insider language such as *autie* to describe themselves. It is inaccurate to say that all people with disabilities prefer one way over another. Person-first language serves as a helpful guideline, because many advocacy groups consider it a respectful way to refer to people.

Q. I do not think the student I work with is smart. This student has a label of ID. How can I presume competence?

A. This person may not perform well on standardized tests of intelligence. However, your responsibility when working with this student is to identify the student's strengths. Keep those strengths in mind. Every person is intelligent in different ways.

CONCLUSION

Remember, labels are not accurate descriptors of people. Children who have disabilities are unique individuals with unlimited potential, just like everyone else (Snow, 2008). This recognition is not only about having a good attitude or believing that all students are smart; it also will allow you to treat, support, and work with all students in ways that promote dignity and respect. In the next chapter, we discuss how the ideas of dignity and respect can help facilitate social relationships.

NOTES

7

Providing Academic Supports

CLEARING A PATH
FOR PEOPLE WITH SPECIAL NEEDS
CLEARS THE PATH FOR EVERYONE!

*"I knew how I wanted academic support to look. When I supervised my staff though . . .
I did not see academic support that aligned with my ideas of best practice."*

—Josh (principal)

Many of us use modifications and adaptations to get through our own days (e.g., setting an alarm to wake up on time). I (Julie) go on a brisk walk before the demands of my day begin; this improves my ability to sit for long periods of time at work. I always set my keys in the same place in the kitchen so that I will not lose them and blame other family members for misplacing them. I use my electronic planner to keep my daily schedule. I always write my daily "to do" list on a large sticky note. I prioritize each item by writing numbers in the left-hand margin of the list. When I clean my house, I set my alarm for 15 minutes, and I race around the house to see how much I can get done before setting the alarm again for the next room. In meetings, I chew gum to keep myself attentive, and I sit close to the front so that I can keep myself from mentally wandering or chatting with my colleagues. The point is this: All people need their environments, time schedules, and behavior modified or adapted to allow them to be successful members of society. This chapter discusses some accommodations, modifications, and adaptations that are made for students with disabilities. We describe general and content-specific strategies and discuss the topic of assistive technology.

It is important for instructional leaders to understand basic modifications and adaptations. This chapter first describes general strategies that will allow for student success, then discusses content-specific ideas and, finally, suggests strategies that can help educators work across all content areas. School leaders can share this chapter with teams of educators who need support or ideas regarding how to include students effectively.

Figure 7.1 shows a general cycle of support, which has been adapted from one developed by Mary Beth Doyle (2008). It is included in this book because this is a very helpful resource to give to paraprofessionals, special educators and general educators. It clearly explains the roles and responsibilities of each person in carrying out instructional responsibilities.

ACCOMMODATIONS, MODIFICATIONS, AND ADAPTATIONS

The following information about the differences between *modifications* and *adaptations* comes from the PEAK Parent Center (n.d.) in Colorado Springs, Colorado. Accommodations and modifications are adaptations made to the environment, curriculum, instruction, or assessment practices that enable students with disabilities to be successful learners and to participate actively with other students in the general education classroom and in schoolwide activities.

Accommodations are changes in how a student gains access to information and demonstrates learning. Accommodations do not substantially change the instructional level, content, or performance criteria. The changes are made to provide a student

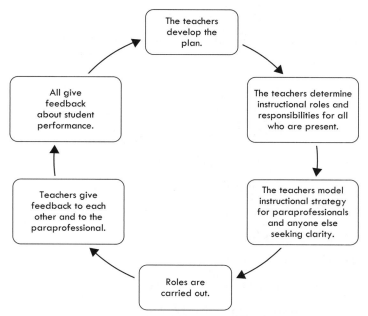

Figure 7.1. General cycle of support. (From Doyle, M.B. [2008]. *The paraprofessional's guide to the inclusive classroom: Working as a team* [3rd ed., p. 58]. Baltimore, MD: Paul H. Brookes Publishing Co.; adapted by permission.)

with equal access to learning and equal opportunity to show what he or she knows and can do. Accommodations can include changes in presentation, response format and procedures, instructional strategies, time and scheduling, environment, equipment, and architecture.

Modifications are changes in what a student is expected to learn. The changes are made to provide a student with opportunities to participate meaningfully and productively along with other students in classroom and school learning experiences. Modifications include changes in instructional level, content, and performance criteria.

The following lists contain examples of accommodations and modifications that can be provided in general education classrooms. IEP teams determine accommodations and modifications that meet the unique and individual needs of their students.

Accommodations

- Test taken orally

- Large-print textbooks

- Additional time to take test

- A locker with an adapted lock

- Weekly home–school communication tool, such as a notebook or daily log book

- Peer support for note-taking

- Lab sheets with highlighted instructions

- Graph paper to assist in organizing and lining up math problems

- Audio-recorded lectures

- Use of a computer for writing

Modifications

- An outline in place of an essay for a major project

- Picture communication symbol choices on tests

- Alternative books or materials on the same theme or topic

- Spelling support from a computerized spell-check program

- Word bank of choices for answers to test questions

- Use of a calculator on a math test

- Film or video supplements in place of text

- Questions reworded using simpler language

- Projects substituted for written reports

- Important words and phrases highlighted

Deciding which accommodations and/or modifications to use is a process that depends on the assignment and needs of each individual student. When the appropriate adaptations are made, all students can have true access to the general education curriculum (PEAK Parent Center, n.d.).

GENERAL STRATEGIES

Principals should promote the general strategies detailed in this section to help ensure students are receiving helpful and appropriate academic support.

Focus on Strengths

When providing support to students, it is easy for educators to become overwhelmed by what a student cannot do. For example, when Julie was providing support to Steven, a third grader with Down syndrome, it was easy to think, "Steven does not read; how am I to help him understand the science content in this chapter?" It helps to reframe your thinking and ask yourself what the student *can* do. Staff should focus on the student's strengths; with Steven, they might think, "Steven is a very social guy. He can easily comprehend big ideas. He is masterful at drawing what he knows and labeling parts. He also can answer questions."

We focused on Steven's strengths of listening, social interaction, and understanding main ideas. When other students were required to quietly read the chapter from the science book, Steven's partner read the chapter aloud. At the end of each section in the text, Steven and his partner were required to say something about the section, and Steven, as he listened, worked on a drawing depicting the big ideas from that section. Steven and his partner then asked each other questions about the section and the drawing. This worked so well for Steven and his partner that the teacher decided to have the entire class read the science text that way for the rest of the year.

One principal we worked with insisted that every meeting about a student focus on the student's strengths. She handed out sticky notes and had each member of the team come up to the chart paper and write down five student strengths, gifts, talents, and abilities. Then as they solved student problems, she requested that the team figure out ways to use the strengths of the student in the solutions. Another principal handed out the Strength and Strategies Profile (see Figure 7.2). She asked team members to list the student's strengths along with useful instructional strategies. This helped the team to begin the conversation with what they already knew.

Ask the Student

If a team is unsure of how to provide support, when to provide support, or how much support to provide, it does not need to make that decision alone. After the team discusses the student's support requirements, team members should consult the student. Many behavioral issues in school occur because the support being given to the student is too invasive.

Keep Expectations High

If a student has a disability, it does not mean that the student cannot complete assignments and projects in the same way as anyone else. Before attempting to modify or alter a student's assignment, teams should ask themselves whether the assignment actually needs any changes. Too often, education professionals overmodify for students or decide to make the same modification for every student with the same disability. Sometimes, the best thing to do for a student is not to change expectations for him or her but, instead, to change the type or level of support.

Break Tasks into Smaller Steps

For some students, it might be useful to break tasks into smaller parts. For example, one student, Chelsea, preferred having a "to do" list posted on her desk for any independent work time. The paraprofessional would write down the big tasks that needed to be completed, and Chelsea would complete them independently and cross out each

Strengths and Strategies Profile

Strengths and strategies profile for _____

Strengths, gifts, interests, and talents	Effective strategies
1.	1.
2.	2.
3.	3.
4.	4.
5.	5.

Figure 7.2. Strengths and Strategies Profile.

From Kluth, P., & Dimon-Borowski, M. (2003). *Strengths and strategies profile.* Retrieved from
http://www.paulakluth.com/wordpress/wp-content/uploads/2011/03/strengthstrategy.pdf; adapted by permission.

In *The Principal's Handbook for Leading Inclusive Schools* by Julie Causton and George Theoharis
(2014, Paul H. Brookes Publishing Co., Inc.)

task. If team members have a student who does not read, they could draw a picture list and have the student cross out each picture as he or she completes each task.

Extend Time on Tasks

Many students can complete the same work as anyone else if they have extra time. In these cases, it may be helpful to slowly decrease the time allotted for certain tasks. Or, if the other students have an hour to complete a test, the student could be allowed to take the test in parts—one part on the first day, the second part on the next.

Present a Limited Amount of Information on a Page

Some students prefer to see less information at once. The layout of information should be clean and free of distraction. Adequate white space, for example, can make an assignment appear less confusing. This modification can easily be made by copying different segments of an assignment onto different pages. In addition, Wite-Out tape helps limit certain distracting information or pictures. Then, when the item is photocopied, the student has less information to wade through. The student can hold an index card and slide it down the page to eliminate the visual clutter of too much text. A word window (i.e., a piece of cardboard with a small rectangular window covered with cellophane that allows students to see one line of text or one word at a time) can also help students eliminate information as they read by themselves.

Offer Support, Do Not Just Give It

Teachers should not assume that a student needs help. If a student is struggling, he or she should be encouraged to ask a peer first. If the student is still struggling, classroom staff should ask, "Can I help you get started?" If the student says, "No," his or her wishes should be respected.

Use a Soft Voice

Receiving support is not always a comfortable thing. It also can be distracting to classmates. Therefore, principals should encourage staff members to use a soft voice when students are working or even to provide silent support. Many teams have found writing things down for students more effective than providing verbal cues.

Make Things Concrete

Many students need concrete examples, such as pictures or videos that support the concepts taught in class. Jill, a paraprofessional with whom we worked, would use downtime to search the school library and Internet for pictures and videos to support learning. The teacher would then incorporate these teaching aids into her mini-lectures and teaching centers. Her use of these visual supports benefited not only the students with disabilities, but everyone in the class.

Teach Organizational Skills to Everyone

It is common for students with and without disabilities to struggle with organization. In one seventh-grade classroom, one team member helped everyone by performing binder checks at the end of each class. She made sure the notes were in the correct color-coded spot as students left the room. This helped not only Adam, who chronically struggled with keeping things organized, but countless others who needed similar support. Another team made a checklist of all the items students needed to take home each day. These lists were made available for any student to use.

Change the Materials

Sometimes, all a student needs for success is a different type of material. A change in type of writing utensil or size or kind of paper can make a substantial difference for a student. For example, Julie used to work with a student named Brett. Every time Brett was expected to write, he would put his head down on the desk or angrily break pencils. The team of teachers and paraprofessionals who supported the classroom met and discussed the potential reasons for Brett's behavior and how they might make writing more pleasant for him. As a result of this conversation, the team decided to let all students choose their writing instruments and paper size. When this choice was offered, Brett chose a black felt-tip marker and a half-sheet of paper. For some reason, the change of materials proved much better for him, and he wrote for longer periods of time. He later explained that he would get nervous if he saw "a whole blank piece of paper" and that he hated "the feel of the pencil on the paper."

Use a Timer

Timers can be useful for students who like to know how long tasks will take or who need help organizing their time. For some students, visual timers, or timers on which the student can actually see how much time is left, can be particularly useful. For Izzy, in the case study that follows, a timer helps him know when a transition is occurring and also gives him an important responsibility.

• • • • • • •

Izzy is a kindergarten student. Whenever transitions in the classroom occur, he has loud tantrums. Because of Izzy's difficulty with transitions, his team decides to use a timer to alert him when the transitions are coming. Izzy's teacher hands him an old track timer and tells him that he is in charge of letting the other students know when it is cleanup time. After first practicing with the timer, Izzy takes his responsibility very seriously. He walks around from group to group, reminding the kindergartners that there are only "5 minutes until cleanup time . . . 4 minutes . . . 3. . . ." He continues to remind his friends until the timer goes off. He then shouts, "Clean up, everyone!"

• • • • • • •

Preteach

Preteaching big ideas such as vocabulary or major concepts can be useful for many students. Preteaching should be done before a concept is "officially" taught to the rest of the class. The teacher or paraprofessional may introduce a concept, term, or idea to a student before the rest of the students learn it. For example, as the students were preparing for a magnet lab, Mr. Marco taught some of the key science vocabulary to Brett before the lesson. Brett entered the magnet lab understanding the terms *attract* and *repel*. This allowed Brett to come into the class prepared and more confident.

Peer Support

One thing to suggest to teams is to utilize peer support, because it is one of the best ways to support students. Teachers can have all the students work in teams or partnerships and tell students that their job is to help each other. However, some caution is necessary regarding peer support. Teachers should not set up "helping relationships"—for example, Sonja always helps Jose. Instead, they should encourage students to help each other—in other words, figure out times when Jose can help Sonja and others in the classroom.

Use Movement

Most students need to move their bodies often. When asking students to memorize discrete concepts or pieces of information, teachers can use visual cues, signs, or movements. Many students who have trouble memorizing can be helped by using movements or visual cues. Teachers can challenge students to come up with their own movements that match the concepts of specific words. For example, one sixth-grade teacher had her class do "spelling aerobics." When spelling words, if the letters were "tall letters" (e.g., *t, l, b*), the students would stand up tall and put their arms up; if letters were "short" (e.g., *o, e, a*), the students would put their hands on their hips; and, if letters hung below the line (e.g., *p, g, q*), the students would touch their toes. For instance, to spell the word *stop,* the students would touch their waists, reach up, touch their waists, and then touch their toes. What makes this particular example so powerful is that the movement is purposeful and connected to the content.

CONTENT-SPECIFIC STRATEGIES

The tables in this section provide a number of modifications and adaptations for different types of content and activities that are commonly used across content areas. This information can be shared with those needing more ideas in various content areas, or can be shared with the entire staff. Instructional leaders should know these types of modifications and how best to use them with students.

Commonly Occurring Activities Across Content Areas

Support can look very different for students in different content areas. Sometimes, a different teacher is responsible for each content area, and this can result in different expectations. Some students prefer certain subjects and perform better in them. For example, Ricky enjoyed music, so he needed almost no support in that class. He would enter the music room, gather his folder and instrument, and be ready to go. In science, he did not seem fond of the teacher or the subject, and he therefore needed more support to get started with tasks. Although a student's support might look different from class to class, teachers use similar activities across different subject areas. Table 7.1 highlights activities that are used commonly across subjects. Teachers may require students to do any number of these things throughout the day. Nonetheless, different students may have difficulty with each of these activities, for different reasons. The considerations listed on the right side of Table 7.1 have proved

Table 7.1. Common activities and supports

When the students are asked to	Consider providing students
Sit and listen	Visuals to look at
	Movement breaks
	An FM system (that amplifies the teacher's voice)
	A rug or mat to help determine where to be
	An object to signify who is speaking (e.g., a talking stick)
	A ball to sit on
	Choice about where to sit
	A focus object for students to hold or manipulate
	A signal to start listening
	The book that is being read
	A topic bag—filled with objects that relate to the content
	A job to do (help another student, write ideas on the board)
Present orally	Choice about the supports necessary
	Note cards
	Visuals
	A handout
	A voice recorder
	A videotape or DVD
	A microphone
	PowerPoint
	A preprogrammed communication device

When the students are asked to	Consider providing students
Take a test	A review of test strategies A review of the information A practice test A double-spaced test Easy questions first A reader for the test A reduced number of choices by eliminating one or two choices In matching, a long column divided into smaller sections A computer As much time as needed An oral exam A performance-based test The option of drawing or labeling Simplified language
Complete worksheets	A word bank Clear directions File folder labels for students to stick answers onto worksheets Highlighted directions Fewer problems or questions Choice about type of writing instrument
Discuss	A talking object Note cards with students' ideas written on them Peer support A preprogrammed communication device with a question on it A piece of paper for drawing ideas or concepts Choice about how to participate in the discussion The text the students are discussing A highlighted section of the text—have the student read and others discuss
Take notes	A lecture outline to complete during the lecture A chart A graphic organizer The teacher's notes from the day before An AlphaSmart laptop computer Choice about how to take notes A copy of the teacher's notes with key words eliminated Lecture notes with pictures Photocopies or carbon copies from another student A laptop computer
Use a computer	A task card for how to start up the program Modified keyboard Enlarged font IntelliKeys assistive keyboard An adjusted delay on the mouse An alphabetical keyboard A large keyboard Choice about what to work on
Read a text	A book on tape Larger print font A highlighter Choral reading Background information about the text Bullets of the main ideas Sticky notes to write questions on

(continued)

Table 7.1.   (*continued*)

When the students are asked to	Consider providing students
Read a text	"Just-right books" Puppets A reading light Choice about what to read
Be organized	Color-coded folders A planner An agenda written on the board Assignments written on the board in the same place Assignments that are already three-hole punched A picture schedule A sticky note on desk of things to do A homework folder A desk check A clock or timer on desk A verbal rehearsal of the schedule A consistent routine
Write	The opportunity to tell a friend his or her story before writing it The opportunity to discuss as a whole group Graphic organizers to use Bullet writing as an alternative Pencil grips The opportunity to dictate the story to an adult or a peer Words on a separate piece of paper for the student to rewrite Stickers for filling in blanks The opportunity to draw instead of write Raised-line paper—so students can feel the lines

Table 7.2.   Content-specific modifications

In this subject	Consider these modifications, adaptations, and accommodations
Reading/language arts	Listen to books on tape/CD. Read with a peer. Follow along with a word window. Read from a computer with headphones. Work with a peer and have him or her summarize. Read enlarged print. Use CCTV (closed circuit TV)—a video magnifier that enlarges the font. Rewrite stories in simpler language. Use books with repetitive texts.
Mathematics	Calculators Touch math (each number has the correct number of dots on the actual number) Hundreds charts Number lines Flash cards Count stickers Manipulatives (e.g., Unifix cubes, counting chips) Worksheet modified with easier-to-read numbers Pictures or visuals Larger cubes Chart paper to keep track of columns Talking calculator Numbered dice instead of dotted dice Real-world problems—problems with students' names in them

In this subject	Consider these modifications, adaptations, and accommodations
Physical education	Different-sized sporting equipment Silent activities (for those who are sensitive to noise) Choice stations Change the size of the court
Art	Choice of materials Bigger/smaller materials Slant board Precut materials Stencils Smocks and aprons with pockets Gloves for kids who do not like to get messy Wiki sticks Posted steps about the process Modified scissors
Science	Hands-on experiences Teacher demonstration A role play Guest speaker Posted steps indicating the process
Social studies	Highlighters or highlighting tape A way to connect the content to self DVDs Visuals Maps A written task card (a card with a step-by-step process on it)
Music	Songs in the student's native language Instruments Signs while singing Rhythms to clap out Tapes/CDs of music to practice at home Music videos to watch

helpful for many students of all abilities. Table 7.2 provides ideas of content-specific modifications.

ASSISTIVE TECHNOLOGY

Assistive technology is any type of technology that helps people with disabilities perform functions that might otherwise be difficult or impossible. As a principal, you may be instrumental in helping to advocate for assistive technology evaluations or approving the purchase of a device for a student. Some background information about assistive technology can be helpful in these decisions. The official definitions of assistive technology are as follows:

> Assistive technology in special education refers to any devices or services that are necessary for a child to benefit from special education or related services or to enable the child to be educated in the least restrictive environment. (IDEA 2004; PL 108-446; § 602 [1]) (34 C.F.R. § 300.308)

The term *assistive technology device* as outlined in IDEA 2004 means any item, piece of equipment, or product system, whether acquired commercially off the shelf, modified, or customized, that is used to increase, maintain or improve functional capabilities of children with disabilities. (20 U.S.C. § 1401 [a][25])

The term *assistive technology service* means any service that directly assists a child with disabilities in the selection, acquisition, or use of an assistive technology device. The term includes:

- The evaluation of the needs of a child with a disability, including a functional evaluation of the child in the child's customary environment;

- Purchasing, leasing, or otherwise providing for the acquisition of assistive technology devices by children with disabilities;

- Selecting, designing, fitting, customizing, adapting, applying, maintaining, repairing, or replacing of assistive technology devices;

- Coordinating and using other therapies, interventions, or services with assistive technology devices, such as those associated with existing education and rehabilitation plans and programs;

- Training or technical assistance for a child with disabilities or, where appropriate, the family of a child with disabilities;

- Training or technical assistance for professionals (including individuals providing education or rehabilitation services), employers, or other individuals who provide services to, employ, or are otherwise substantially involved in the major life functions of individuals with disabilities. (20 U.S.C. § 1401 [a][26])

Assistive technology includes mobility devices (e.g., walkers, wheelchairs), software, keyboards with large keys, software enabling students who are blind to use computers, or text telephones that enable students who are deaf to talk on telephones. A student who struggles with the fine motor skills involved with writing might use an AlphaSmart device, and a student who struggles to communicate might type his or her ideas into an iPad, which then speaks the ideas aloud. If a student uses assistive technology, team members should learn as much as they can about the specific technology. If possible, the principal should provide training on the technology so that team members can assist the student in using the device, programming it, or fixing it if necessary. See the Chapter 7 Appendix for a list of useful web sites and resources for assistive technology.

Supervision Suggestions

As a principal, you will supervise staff to provide modifications or adaptations to students and help them navigate the academic terrain of schooling. Therefore, it is helpful to have information about how to best supervise and support. One critical supervisory issue is identifying who is providing or creating the modifications and adaptations. In many schools, the task of modification and adaptation is wrongly relegated to the paraprofessional working with an individual student. It is important to remember that the No Child Left Behind Act of 2001 (PL 107-110) requires paraprofessionals to work with students "under the direct supervision of a certified staff member." The law stipulates that it is not the responsibility of paraprofessionals to decide the best modifications or adaptations to use with students. Instead, they should be given written plans. Therefore, certified teachers should write the lessons, and paraprofessionals should carry out and take data on the implementation of the modifications.

TWENTY-ONE WAYS TO USE A STICKY NOTE

We once knew a paraprofessional who wrote the student she supported a positive note on a sticky note every day. The student brought that note home and read it with his parents. The purpose of those notes was to provide only positive comments to the student. These kind notes really helped the student feel good about his performance at school. Sticky notes are amazingly versatile. We suggest, during a staff meeting, that you challenge your staff to think of as many ways as they can to use sticky notes to support students academically. Figure 7.3 shows 21 great ideas.

- As an individual agenda
- As a to-do list
- For a positive note in a pocket
- To mark page numbers
- As a reading guide
- To highlight sections of text
- To place under the directions
- To write questions to the students in their reading books
- As a written reminder about behavior
- As a way to monitor hand raising (every time students raise their hands and answer, they mark the note)
- To cover up sections of a worksheet
- As a word bank (so students don't have to write but can, instead, place a word in the blank)
- For students who have a lot to say and blurt out a lot—have them write their questions on sticky notes and select one or two to ask
- To add ideas to a brainstormed list
- For students to give feedback to each other on projects or papers
- To label parts of a diagram
- To create a matching game
- To put students into groups
- For students to write questions or comments and then give to their teacher as a ticket out the door
- To ask a question to a peer, such as, "Do you want to sit with me at lunch?"
- To summarize the main idea of a lesson, story, or activity

Figure 7.3. Twenty-one ways to use a sticky note.

COMMONLY ASKED QUESTIONS ABOUT ACADEMIC SUPPORTS

Q. One student asks a special education teacher to "go away" when she works with him. We cannot just let him sit there and fail. What should we do?

A. Listen to the student. If a student requests that someone not work with him or her, that person should not support the student at that time. Instead, the special education teacher should figure out how he or she might provide support without being physically next to the student. The lists of support strategies in this chapter should be helpful.

Q. I've realized that the paraprofessionals are not receiving written plans and they do not have any time to meet with their teachers. How should I proceed?

A. This is a common and major problem. Sit down with the schedules of paraprofessionals and teachers and carve out some common communication time.

Q. My teachers are beginning to co-plan and co-deliver instruction, but I notice that most teams are using very traditional teaching—primarily large group and mainly lecture style. What do I do now?

A. The fact that teachers are co-planning and co-teaching is a great success. That should be celebrated. It is now important to help instructional teams broaden their skills. There are many ways to help teachers learn active learning, adaption, or differentiation strategies. Consider engaging in ongoing learning or inquiry groups around these topics, in which teachers learn a handful of new strategies, go and implement them, and then come back and discuss.

CONCLUSION

As a principal, although you do not often provide direct support to students, it is still very helpful to become familiar with the multitude of ways students can be supported. Careful support is critical when providing support to students during academic work time. Teaching teams should take the time to discuss the types of support necessary to enable students to learn certain subjects or perform certain activities, how to fade support, and how to best adapt material and instruction across curricular areas—it is time well spent. It is interesting to note that, when teams make these changes for specific students, they can end up making improvements to teaching for all students. See the cartoon (at the beginning of the chapter) for an illustration of this concept. This chapter has focused on the many ways you can use strategies to support academics. The next chapter highlights behavioral support strategies.

NOTES

_____

_____

_____

_____

_____

_____

_____

_____

_____

_____

_____

_____

_____

_____

_____

_____

_____

_____

_____

_____

_____

_____

_____

_____

_____

_____

7

Appendix

USEFUL WEB SITES AND
RESOURCES FOR ASSISTIVE TECHNOLOGY

AbleData
http://www.abledata.com

AccessIT: The National Center on Accessible Information Technology in Education
http://www.washington.edu/accessit/index.html

Alliance for Technology Access
http://www.ataccess.org

CAST: Transforming Education through Universal Design for Learning
http://www.cast.org

CATEA: Center for Assistive Technology and Environmental Access
http://www.assistivetech.net

National Center to Improve Practice in Special Education Through Technology,
  Media and Materials
http://www2.edc.org/NCIP

NATRI: National Assistive Technology Research Institute
http://natri.uky.edu

RehabTool
http://www.rehabtool.com/at.html

University of Connecticut Center for Students with Disabilities
http://www.csd.uconn.edu

8

Providing
Behavioral Supports

CONSIDERING HER STUDENTS WITHOUT
DISABILITIES, MRS. BAKER
REALIZES DAVID'S UNUSUAL
BEHAVIORS AREN'T THAT UNUSUAL.

"I spend so much time dealing with student behavior. My office is like a revolving door."

—Michelle (principal)

"My staff thinks I am soft on behavior. I try to build a relationship with each student who is sent to my office. The staff wants the students to feel the consequences of being sent to the principal. There is an attitude of remove and punish, remove and punish. We know that does not work to change behavior, and I think it is all so much more complex."

—Dale (principal)

Once we were giving a presentation to a large group of teachers. We asked them to list the most challenging behaviors they had seen among their students. The teachers thought about it for a while and then shared their lists with us as we wrote their ideas on chart paper. The lists included swearing, fighting, yelling, shutting down, becoming silent, running out of the room, hitting, and injuring oneself (e.g., biting one's own arm).

We then asked this same group of teachers whether they ever had participated in those behaviors themselves. We told them to raise their hands if they ever had sworn, fought, yelled, shut down, become silent, run out of a room, hit someone, or done anything to hurt themselves. The sound of nervous laughter filled the room as almost everyone raised their hands. This is no reflection about that particular group of teachers. Most people, on occasion, behave in ways that would be considered challenging or concerning. When we then asked the teachers to distinguish the students' challenging behaviors from their own behavior, one teacher responded, in a half-joking manner, "When I have bad behavior, I have a darn good reason!" Guess what? So do students.

We next asked the group to think about what they needed when they engaged in bad behavior. They brainstormed this list: a hug, time away, someone to listen, a glass of wine, a nap, a cool-off period, changing the subject, talking to someone. We consider this a good list. Many of those things also help both of us calm down when we are angry or upset. Notice, however, not only what they suggested, but also what was *not* suggested. No teacher reported needing a sticker chart. No one said they needed to be lectured to or be kicked out of the room. Instead, like most people, these adults needed support, comfort, and calm, gentle understanding. Guess what? Students need that, too.

Given the realities of your job, you almost certainly work with students who have challenging behaviors. These may range from relatively nonconfrontational behaviors such as skipping class or shutting down to more significant or externalizing behaviors such as fighting with other classmates, running out of the school, or hurting oneself. This chapter begins with a discussion of typical responses to challenging behaviors and an overview of positive behavior supports. Then, we present a series of recommendations of what to do before, during, and after students demonstrate these types of challenging behaviors. At the end of the chapter, we answer some commonly asked questions.

THE TYPICAL RESPONSE TO CHALLENGING BEHAVIOR

Herb Lovett, a researcher who was at the Institute on Disability at the University of New Hampshire, described the typical response to challenging behavior:

Our initial response to an unwanted behavior is to react, to correct what we perceive to be unacceptable, inappropriate behavior. The thinking behind this perception is that the person exhibiting the behavior has lost control and that those who are in charge—in control—are responsible for regaining it through the application of methods and technologies specifically designed for this purpose. (1996, p. 136)

The major problem with this type of response is that, when the chosen method of control does not work, the teacher or paraprofessional tends to become frustrated and, consequently, use more punitive methods for control. The intentions backfire and, through a need to control and correct, teachers and paraprofessionals often create formidable barriers that further alienate them from those they are supposed to support and teach (Lovett, 1996). What follow are ideas and suggestions to move away from these typical responses to behavior toward a much more humanistic method of supporting students.

POSITIVE BEHAVIOR SUPPORT

Janney and Snell provided a useful explanation of positive behavior supports:

Positive behavioral supports have been developed as a movement away from the traditional mechanistic and even aversive behavior management practices that were being applied to students with disabilities. This approach emphasizes the use of collaborative teaming and problem-solving processes to create supports that stress prevention and remediation of problem behaviors through the provision of effective educational programming and the creation of a supportive environment. (2008, p. 2)

The basic tenets of positive behavior support are as follows (Carr et al., 2002; Janney & Snell, 2008):

1. Behavior is learned and can change.

2. Intervention is based on studying the behavior.

3. The intervention emphasizes prevention and teaching new behaviors.

4. Outcomes are personally and socially valued.

5. Intervention requires comprehensive, integrated supports.

Note that positive behavior supports require a team approach. One person alone should not be expected to design a positive behavior support program. However, as the school leader it is essential that you model and expect a positive behavior approach, so clearly understanding the basic tenets of the program is important.

PROACTIVE BEHAVIOR MANAGEMENT

Most challenging behavior can be avoided or managed by thinking ahead. Thinking ahead involves determining what works for the student.

• • • • • • •

Gabe, a student with autism, has a very difficult time with changes in his schedule. He needs to know when transitions will occur. If he is surprised by a change in the schedule, he hides in his locker, paces, or runs around the room. One way to avoid this issue is to prepare Gabe for each day's schedule. The teaching team does this by having a peer greet Gabe's bus in the morning. Gabe and his peer then walk to the room together, and when they reach the classroom, they review the agenda for the day. Gabe also has an individual copy of the schedule in his planner. This strategy represents one of the most successful ways to prepare Gabe for the day ahead and to reduce his anxiety about the schedule.

• • • • • • •

Building a Relationship

Lovett highlighted the importance of relationships and connections as more central than anything else related to supporting students behaviorally:

> A positive approach [to behavior] invites people to enter into the same sort of relationship that most of us have and treasure: ongoing, with mutual affection and regard. In such relationships, we all make mistakes, are all in some ways inadequate and yet it is not the level of success that is the ongoing commitment. In the context of relationships, the success and failure of our work becomes harder to assess because the key elements no longer involve simply quantity but the more complex issues of quality. We professionals have routinely overlooked the significance of relationships. (1996, p. 137)

Getting to know your students and learning what they enjoy can be a truly helpful way to address challenging behaviors. "Creating a suitable level of rapport with students is an absolute essential prerequisite for helping students behave" (Knoster, 2008, p. 25).

• • • • • • •

Lisa, a paraprofessional working with Connie, a high school student with Down syndrome, was having a difficult time getting to know Connie. They just were not clicking. Lisa decided to go to Connie's house on the weekend to get to know her better.

Lisa asked her teammates and Connie's parents for their consent. Connie showed Lisa all around her house and introduced her to her brother and grandmother. Most important, Lisa met Connie's dog, Champ. Lisa indicated that this home visit was one of the most important ways to break down Connie's walls and for them to begin to trust one another. When Connie was interviewed about her relationship with Lisa, Connie said, "I trust her. We get through the good and bad times together. Without that, I do not know what I would do."

• • • • • • •

Clearly, Lisa created an opportunity for Connie to trust her. She achieved this through a home visit and by continuing to be a trustworthy figure in Connie's life. However, there are many different ways to form relationships and to let students know that you trust them and that they can trust you. Some different methods include generally being there for the student if he or she needs you, having fun with the student, learning about the student's home life without making a home visit, seeing the same movies that the student enjoys, participating in the same activities the student likes, and talking to the student about his or her friends and hobbies. The next section discusses additional ways to build rapport each day with students.

How Do I Help Staff Build Rapport with Students?

Latham (1999) provided steps for parents to build rapport with their children. While many teachers, staff, and administrators have great abilities to build relationships with a range of students, there are always a significant number who struggle in this area. These steps have been modified for staff to use with students and are included here:

1. Demonstrate age-appropriate touch (high-five, hand shake), facial expressions (reflect the nature of the situation), tone of voice (e.g., your voice also should match the situation), and body language (e.g., appear relaxed, keep your arms open, be attentive, look at the student).

2. Ask open-ended questions (e.g., "What are you doing after school?" "What was your favorite part of the movie?").

3. Listen while the student is speaking. Ideally, talk less than the student (do not interrupt or change the subject).

4. Demonstrate the use of empathetic statements. Act like a mirror and reflect the child's feelings by expressing your understanding and caring.

5. Ignore nuisance behavior and let the little stuff slide.

Matching Instructional Practices to Student Strengths

One of the simplest ways to support students' positive behavior is to match instructional techniques to student strengths. For example, when a student who is a successful artist is allowed to draw his or her ideas during the social studies lecture, the student is more likely to be engaged and have positive behavior. As a leader, you might not have a lot of control regarding how the hour-by-hour instruction is planned. However, we know that leaders play an essential role in helping teachers integrate new instructional techniques that support student learning. By engaging in proactive and positive problem solving, trying out ideas, and putting new plans in place, you can help your teams use alternative approaches that others in the school can try as well. You can always suggest new ideas. Never underestimate your power and creativity in supporting the students with whom you work.

• • • • • • •

Sue (a paraprofessional) supports a student (Alex) who needs to move often. Sue asks the general education teacher whether they can put chart paper on the wall and have all students stand and use markers to do a brainstorming activity instead of doing it at their desks. The teacher is willing to try it. Alex is more successful, and the other students seem to really enjoy this approach.

Before this, Alex was considered naughty because he never sat still. He was always out of his seat, wiggling and moving. What Sue sensed was that Alex's misbehavior indicated a learning preference (a bodily kinesthetic learning preference). Sue had an idea for putting more movement into Alex's learning.

· · · · · · ·

Knowing and understanding how students misbehave can help staff identify what the students need. Research has demonstrated that taking advantage of students' strengths decreases negative behavior and increases on-task behaviors (Kornhaber, Fierros, & Veenema, 2004). See the following examples:

- If students are constantly moving or are bodily kinesthetic learners, they need more movement during instruction. For example, EunYoung needs to move during instruction. So, when the teacher reads aloud to the class, EunYoung is allowed to sit in a rocking chair. The teachers in EunYoung's class let the students sit however they like during certain class activities.

- If students are continually talking or are interpersonal learners, they need more interaction during learning. For example, Gwen works best when she is able to talk with peers. So, before writing a journal entry, she is given a few minutes to talk to a friend about what she plans to write.

- If students are constantly singing or are musically gifted, they need more music in school. Lucy enjoys music, so the teacher uses music during writing workshops. The music helps Lucy stay focused, and other students also enjoy it.

- If students enjoy making connections to their own lives or are intrapersonal learners, they need more time during school to make personal connections to the content. For example, Jerry enjoys making personal connections. So, during the *Little House on the Prairie* unit, Jerry's assignment is to determine how each of the settlers is like him and different from him.

- If students draw or doodle or are spatial learners, you can make art part of the learning process. For example, Rubin likes to draw. So, while he listens to a mini-lecture about cellular division, Rubin has the option of drawing the concepts.

- If a student enjoys mathematical calculations or is highly logical, you can use math and logic to strengthen the student's learning in other subjects. For example, Jorge loves math and struggles during English. So, the paraprofessional has Jorge make Venn diagrams, time lines, and graphs about the characters in *Romeo and Juliet*. This helps him keep track of all of the characters and, during discussion, he shares his charts with other students to help them remember the details of the book.

Set Up the Environment in a Way that Promotes Positive Behavior

Have you ever walked into a classroom that felt controlled and stiff? Have you ever been in a learning environment that you wanted to escape from? What type of learning environment promotes learning? The following list offers ideas to help promote a more comfortable classroom environment.

- Arrange desks in a way that allows for easy student interaction. A circle of desks grouped into tables is more likely to promote interaction.

- Seat students with disabilities in different locations in the room. Do not group students with disabilities together.

- Create a calm, relaxed place in which students feel comfortable moving around and engaging with others.

- Create structure by posting the agenda or daily schedule.

- Do not isolate any student by seating him or her in a separate location.

- Make it feel like a space for students by adorning the walls with student work.

- Have music playing softly in the background at times.

- If students are expected to sit on the floor, a soft, carpeted place will make them feel more comfortable.

- If a student struggles with personal space, have all students sit on carpet squares.

- If a student does not like to be called on in class without warning, set up a system to let the student know when the teacher will call on him or her.

Although principals are often called after challenging behaviors have started, a better use of principal time and energy is in helping create comfortable and relaxed environments so that problematic behaviors are less likely.

Meet Students' Needs

All human beings require certain things to be happy and, therefore, well behaved. These things have been called *universal desires* (Lovett, 1996). Autonomy, relationships, interdependence, safety, trust, pleasure, joy, communication, self-esteem, belonging, self-regulation, and accomplishment are needs for all human beings. Helping students meet these needs is essential to creating learning environments in which students feel comfortable and safe; such feelings, in turn, help resolve behavioral issues.

Autonomy   *Autonomy* means the right or power to govern oneself or to be self-determined. To help students feel autonomous, provide choices and allow them to make as many decisions as possible. Examples include choice in seat location, whom to sit by, the materials to use for a project, the topic of a project, the type of writing instrument, whether to have something modified, and what to eat. Allowing students more choices enhances their ability to make decisions and become independent people.

Relationships and Interdependence　Student relationships are deeply important. Students need to be allowed to have relationships and connections with their peers. Opportunities should be created for students to help one another. When these needs are not met, students will invariably try to gain each other's attention. This bid for attention occurs in a variety of ways: it may be through hitting, tapping, or pestering. Students might also seem lonely and choose to sit by themselves. They may seem angry and try to get removed from certain settings through challenging behaviors.

Safety and Trust　Creating a safe, trusting relationship with your staff requires you to follow through when you say you are going to do something. Demonstrating that you can be trusted will serve you well in the long run. The same holds true for developing relationships with students—both your and staff members' relationships with students. Students need to feel that the adults at school are not trying to punish or hurt any students. It is vital that staff keep their promises to students. "Many people who engage in difficult behaviors have too much experience with broken promises" (Pitonyak, 2010, p. 18). The principal should work with teachers and paraprofessionals to continually send the message that they are there to be trusted to help and support, not to punish and manage. This requires an ongoing effort to avoid removing students from the learning environment. Every time a student is removed for a time-out or a brief stint in the hall, a clear message is sent to that student. The message is, "You are not welcome here. Your membership in this community is contingent on your behavior." This tends to create a vicious cycle: Students feel that they do not belong, and they act in ways to demonstrate such feelings; if they are removed, their suspicions are reinforced.

Pleasure and Joy　All students need pleasure and joy in their learning environments. When helping to solve problems regarding supporting a student, ask, "How often does this student experience pleasure or joy in the classroom?" "How often does this student laugh or have fun with others?" "How can more time be devoted to pleasure and joy in the environment?" Too often, schools and classrooms become places where no one wants to be—neither the students nor the adults. Keep in mind that it is important to consider ways to increase joy and happiness for students and staff.

Communication　All students deserve the right to communicate their needs and wants. Once, when Julie was observing students in a classroom, the teacher asked about the weather and date. One student using a communication device pushed a button to make the device say, "I know the answer." He pushed the button again and pushed it three more times during the morning meeting. He was never called on to answer. It seemed that the teacher was beginning to feel frustrated by the noise of the device, and eventually she walked over and took the device away from him. He later found the device and pushed the button to make the device say, "I feel sad." This story illustrates an important point. Communication is not something to be earned and taken away. Any attempt to communicate should be honored, because all people need to be heard.

If students do not believe they are being heard, they will attempt to communicate their thoughts, feelings, and needs through their behavior. Students will assert their own independence, behave in certain ways to receive pleasure and joy, act out when they do not feel safe or need to communicate something, and simply act out to create more pleasure and joy in their lives. Purposefully creating such opportunities is essential to helping students avoid negative behavior. Students might be communicating something such as "I am lonely," "I do not feel safe," or "I do not know how to tell you what I need." The behavior they exhibit might not be easy to identify as communication, but it is important to remember that all behavior is communication. Part of your job as school leader is to help your staff figure out what students are attempting to communicate in their behavior. See Table 8.1 for suggestions to help staff give students more of what they need.

Table 8.1.   Give them what they need

For students who	Give them	For example
Talk a lot	More opportunity to talk	Talk walk, think pair share, debate, turn and talk
Move a lot	More opportunity to move	Stand and write, do graffiti, write Michelangelo style, dance party, back to back
Want to lead	More opportunity to lead	Line leader, paper passer, helper, pointer
Appear shy	More support with social interactions	Write ideas before joining the group, clock partners
Are resistant	More choices	Choice of writing utensil, type or color of paper, types of manipulatives
Have tantrums	Time to calm down, and then a plan when finished	"When you are ready, let's write down your first step."
Bully others	More opportunities to strengthen friendships	Tables at lunch based on interest, supported conversations with peers
Shut down	More ways to express frustration	"I need a break" card, a white board to write feelings down
Make noise	Opportunities to make noise	A mouse pad to drum on, repetitive lines in read aloud
Interrupt	Opportunities to share during lessons	Turn and talk, say something, social break, cooperative learning groups
Have issues with assigned seating	Opportunities to select the best way to work	Use a clipboard on the floor, use a music stand, write Michelangelo style, do graffiti

Ask Yourself: "What Does This Person Need?"

When addressing behavior issues, have staff make a plan for each student to help him or her receive more of the things that will fulfill his or her needs. For example, if staff believe a student needs more choice, they should provide the student more choice—not take choice away.

We are aware that this recommendation contradicts most behavior systems and plans. Many people believe that if they give others what they need, they will just act out more. The opposite, however, is true. If your staff help meet students' needs, the students will not need to misbehave more to get what they want (Lovett, 1996; Pitonyak, 2010).

Table 8.2. Asking new questions about behavior

Challenging behavior	Deficit thinking questions	New questions
Constantly moving	Why won't Zoey sit crisscross during read-aloud time?	How can I restructure the read-aloud experience so Zoey can move and learn simultaneously?
Talking	Why is Liam interrupting during math when I am trying to teach a lesson?	How can I create interactive discussions during lessons, sending the message that meaningful participation is valued?
Singing	Why does Mia continue to hum during reading workshop when I have told her that this is an independent work time?	What sensory supports can I make available to Mia so that she is productive during reading workshop but also does not distract others in our learning community?
All about me	Why does James continue to talk about activities and things he has done outside of school when we're exploring new science topics?	How can James share his background knowledge about science to motivate those around him? How can being a "science expert" support James's reading of nonfiction texts?
Shutting down	Why does Jazz hide her face when unfamiliar adults speak to her?	How can we support Jazz to develop relationships and interact effectively with new adults?
Asking why	Why does Ashley constantly challenge me by asking "why"?	What research opportunities can be built into learning experiences that allow Ashley to develop intricate knowledge about the "why" of concepts being studied?
Challenging or arguing	Why does Isaiah frequently bicker with classmates during playground time?	What social skills could be taught to allow Isaiah to play and engage in cooperative learning groups effectively?
Running out	Why does Aiden scream and run out of the class?	Does Aiden have an effective communication system? What does this behavior communicate? Are the academic tasks differentiated to meet Aiden's needs?
Engaging in self-injurious behavior	Why does Chloe pick her fingers until they bleed and do other things that just hurt herself?	What is the function of this behavior? Did I ask Chloe why she does this?
Being rough with support staff	Why does Jack swat the paraprofessional when she is just trying to reexplain the directions?	Is the paraprofessional providing too much academic and social support in close proximity? How can we fade support? How can we teach Jack to ask for support when he needs it?

Here are some great questions for team members to ask themselves:

- What might this person need?

- Does this person need more pleasure and joy in his or her school day?

- Does this person need more choice or control over what happens to him or her?

- Does this person need to feel more as if he or she belongs?

- Does this person need more relationships and interdependence?

- Does this person need more autonomy?

- Does this person need more access to communication?

First, work with your teams to determine each student's needs, and then to determine avenues to meet those needs. Table 8.2 provides some *new* questions to help teams think differently about behavior.

WEATHERING THE STORM

When confronting challenging behavior, school personnel often react by imposing consequences, threatening to impose consequences, removing rewards, or ignoring the behavior; in some instances, school personnel might force students to behave. Forcing a student to behave might involve physically moving a student or providing hand-over-hand assistance.

We remember watching one student engaging in difficult behavior in a classroom. The student was supposed to be working with the occupational therapist with some Unifix cubes. Instead, the student began running and throwing the cubes at the OT. The OT responded by saying, "If you do not stop, I will write your name on the board and you will lose recess time." The student did not stop. The OT walked over and wrote the student's name on the board in large letters. The student became loud and continued running around. The OT then put a checkmark next to the student's name as more Unifix cubes rained down on her head. She eventually said, "You are going to the time-out room!" She brought the student, kicking and screaming, to the time-out room, where he spent 2 hours, screaming, until he eventually fell asleep.

These types of situations are very difficult; you may have witnessed similar situations. There might not be easy solutions in these cases, but educators often jump to threats and isolation as their first line of defense. Researchers have determined that, although negative reinforcement may stop a behavior in the short term, it is not an effective or humane way to stop the behavior for the long term (Kohn, 2006).

We admit that it is easy for us to suggest alternatives; we were not the one who was frustrated by the behavior of the student who ran around throwing things at the therapist. Nonetheless, consider some different reactions the therapist might have had. How do you think the interaction between the OT and the boy throwing cubes might have changed had the therapist done any of the following?

- Walked over to the student and quietly asked, "What do you need right now?"

- Given the student a piece of paper and said, "Draw for me what is wrong."

- Calmly asked the student whether he needed a break or a drink of water

- Asked the student to help clean up the mess

- Changed the activity entirely and asked the student to help her get ready for the next activity

- Interpreted the student's behavior and said, "Are you finished?" or "Something seems wrong; can you help me understand what it is?"

Had the OT responded with any of these reactions, we doubt that the student would have ended up in the time-out room with so much instructional time lost and at a major personal cost to the student and the OT.

Alfie Kohn, a thoughtful researcher on rewards and punishments, suggested that rewards and punishments "work" in the short term. However, educators need to ask themselves, "Work to do what?" and "At what cost?" When educators think big about what they want for their students in life, they might think they want all their students to be self-reliant, responsible, socially skilled, caring people. Rewards and punishments produce only temporary compliance. They buy obedience (Kohn, 2006). They do not help anybody develop an intrinsic sense of responsibility. In your own life, think of a task that you do not enjoy doing. For example, I (Julie) personally dislike taking out the garbage. Now, think for a moment: What if every time I took out the garbage, someone said to me, "Good job taking out the garbage, Julie"? Would that be more motivating? It wouldn't be for me. Sometimes, things people think are rewarding are actually not.

All Behavior Communicates Something

It is important to understand that all behavior communicates something. If a student is engaging in challenging behavior, ask yourself and your staff, "What might this student be communicating?" Once you have made your best guess at what the student needs, try to meet that student's needs. We watched a paraprofessional do this beautifully. A student, Hayden, was continually tapping a classmate, Sarah, on the back; the tapping seemed to bother Sarah. Instead of assuming that Hayden was trying to be obnoxious or to get attention, the paraprofessional interpreted Hayden's behavior as an attempt to interact with a friend. The paraprofessional whispered to Hayden, "Do you want to move closer and talk with Sarah? One way to start the conversation is to just say 'Hi.'" Hayden moved closer and said, "Hi," and the conversation went on from there.

Some useful ways to interpret what a student is communicating include the following:

- *Ask the student.* Say, "I see you are doing *X*; what do you want me to know?" or "It must mean something when you bang your head. What does it mean?"

- *Watch and learn.* Record everything the student does before and after a behavior. Meet with the team and try to determine what the student is attempting to gain from behaving this way.

- *Attribute positive motives.* One of the most important things is to consider what you believe about a particular child. Attribute the best possible motive consistent with the facts (Kohn, 2006). Assume that the student does not have malicious intent; the student probably is trying to get his or her needs met or to communicate something.

We saw the strategy of attributing positive motives handled well in a hallway setting. A girl ran into a teacher in the hall, and the girl's backpack hit the teacher. The teacher bent down and began yelling at the student: "You gotta stop messing around. If you keep this up, I will call your mother." (Trust us, that is not the good part!) A paraprofessional who was walking with the class said, "I do not think she meant to run into you. I saw what happened; she was walking along and talking with her friend. She didn't see you stop, and she didn't mean to run into you."

This situation can be filtered through two different lenses. When you attribute the best possible motive consistent with the facts, you often see things in a positive and, possibly, more accurate light. This positive spin opens the door for more humanistic approaches to behavior. On the other hand, when behavior is interpreted as malicious or mean-spirited, it is all too easy to respond in a similar way.

Have you ever been out of control? What do you need when you are out of control? Most people need someone to listen, someone to talk to, someone to not give advice; sometimes, an out-of-control person may need a nap or some time away. When students are in the heat of the moment, that is when they often need the most caring, from a calm person. They need an adult or trusted person who is safe, calm, and cool and who will gently, calmly provide support.

What students do *not* need in the heat of the moment (or ever, for that matter) is to be ignored; to be yelled at; to be treated with hostility, sarcasm, or public humiliation; or to be forcefully removed from the situation.

Paula Kluth, an expert on behavior management (particularly with students who have autism), offered this advice:

> When a student is kicking, biting, banging her head, or screaming, she is most likely miserable, confused, scared or uncomfortable. The most effective and the most human response at this point is to offer support; to act in a comforting manner, and to help the person relax and feel safe. Teaching can come later. In a crisis, the educator must listen, support and simply be there. (2005, p. 2)

How Are the Other Students Behaving?

When students with disabilities are supported by special education staff, they invariably are under extra scrutiny. This sometimes leads to behavioral expectations that are more stringent for students with disabilities than for other students. We see this very frequently in classrooms. In one case, we heard a teacher tell a student to sit up tall while working, although two other students in the room were sleeping and one other student was crawling on the floor. Observe how the other students are expected to behave; the student being supported should not be expected to perform at a higher behavioral standard. The cartoon at the beginning of this chapter illustrates this point.

Nothing Personal

As a special educator, Julie dealt with her fair share of challenging behaviors. As a principal, George certainly did as well. A challenge we both faced was not to take anything personally. We have had students who were particularly good at figuring out our buttons and pushing them (or so we thought). The best advice we heard was to remember that the offensive behavior was "nothing personal." Many of the students we have worked with invariably had challenging behavior. They all were learning how to manage their own behavior. At times, we each told ourselves, "It is not personal. Even though this student has just called me a name, it is not about me right now." The challenging behaviors of some students are functions of their disabilities. Consider helping your staff understand the following important point: Just as you would not get angry with a student who was having difficulty walking or reading—because you would assume that this was a function of the student's disability—you should not get angry with students who are struggling to behave. The best, most humane way to respond in these situations is to be helpful and supportive.

Think Like a Parent

Remember that every student is someone's child. When faced with a student's challenging behavior, imagine that you are someone who deeply loves the student. Try to imagine what it would be like if you had watched the child grow and learn from infancy onward; how would you react from that perspective? How might you react if it were your son, daughter, niece, or nephew? If you help your staff members learn to react from a position of love and acceptance, they are much more likely to respond with kindness and humanity than with punishment and control.

HELPING STUDENTS TO MOVE ON

If a student has just had a significant behavioral outburst, he or she may be embarrassed, tired, or still holding on to negative feelings. It is important to help students move past these experiences. After an outburst, a team member should let the student know that the crisis is over, validate his or her feelings, and help him or her move on. The phrases listed in Table 8.3 are offered as a guide to help you and your teams think about how to talk to students to get them beyond emotional crises—but the phrases should not be memorized and repeated. The most important thing is for all the adults who interact with students to use a calm, loving tone of voice as they communicate with the students.

After the outburst, team members should help the student repair any damage. When an adult makes a mistake or loses his or her temper, he or she first needs to repair the damage. Once, while giving a presentation, we made the mistake of using someone in the audience as an example. We did not think it would embarrass that person, but we subsequently learned that it had. We felt awful and had to repair the damage. We did so by writing a note of apology. Writing an apology note might not be the best way for a student to repair the damage after a behavioral outburst; the point is that someone working with the student should help the student identify what might help fix the situation and involve him or her in repairing it. The solution should match the problem. For example, if a student knocks books off a shelf during a tantrum, the best solution is to have the student pick up the books. If a student rips up his or her artwork, the solution might be to have the student either tape it together or create a new piece. If a student yells at a peer, a solution might be to have him or her write an apology note, draw an apology picture, or simply say, "I am sorry." The repair suggested should not be bigger than the problem. The main goal should be to get students back to work in a timely manner.

Table 8.3. How to communicate with students after a behavior issue occurs

To communicate to a student	You might respond with
That the crisis is over	"You are done with that now." "The problem is done." Having the student draw the problem and then having him or her cross it out to signify that the situation has ended
That you validate this student's feelings	"It is okay to feel that way." "I understand that was hard for you." "Now it is over." "I am sorry that was so hard for you." "I can tell you were really frustrated, angry, or upset." Drawing a picture of the student and then drawing thought bubbles over the student's head and asking the student to help you identify what he or she was thinking and feeling
That it is time to move on	"What do you need now?" "What can I help you with to get you back to work?" "Do you want to take a rest and prepare to get yourself back together?" "Would you prefer to get right back to work?" "Draw for me what you need right now."

COMMONLY ASKED QUESTIONS ABOUT BEHAVIORAL SUPPORTS

Q. If a student is not punished, will he or she simply repeat the behavior?

A. We do not believe in adding on a punishment. In fact, much research has been done on the use of time-outs and punishments. This research suggests that punishments work in the short term but have long-term negative effects on students (Kohn, 2006). The research also suggests that serious punishments, such as suspension, do not correct behavior but end up being predictors of more suspensions.

Q. One of my students is not aggressive toward peers—only toward adults. What does that indicate?

A. This type of aggression usually indicates a problem with the type or intensity of support being provided. Students often lash out at paraprofessionals or teachers who make them feel different or uncomfortable because of the support being given. For example, we observed a 12-year-old girl who was being aggressive toward the paraprofessional. We noticed that the paraprofessional was providing intensive support by sitting next to the girl. The paraprofessional was also using a technique called "spidering" (crawling the hand up the back of the student's hair). The student seemed embarrassed and uncomfortable with that type and level of support. When the paraprofessional moved away from the student, the aggression stopped.

Q. I have told a number of paraprofessionals to provide extensive support to a specific student and never to leave the student's side. I understand that this can be embarrassing to the student, and I have seen this extensive support cause certain problems. What should I do?

A. Educators have to provide the type of support that the student actually needs, not support that has a negative impact on social and academic engagement. If your school is seeing these issues, work with your teams and discuss when it might be appropriate to fade or rethink intensive support: What would fading look like for this student? What other types of support can be in place to allow for student success?

Q. Should a student leave the room if he or she is distracting other students?

A. Having the student leave the room should be the absolute last resort. Teams should instead try many different stay-put supports. The student should be helped to stay in the environment for all of the reasons mentioned in this chapter. If a student leaves every time he or she makes a noise, that student learns that

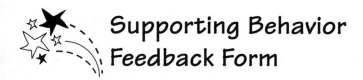

Supporting Behavior
Feedback Form

Class:	Date:	Time:
Lesson/content:	Teachers: 1. 2.	
	Other adults present:	

	Look for:	Evidence:	Descriptions:
Communicative nature of behavior	Teachers make attempts to understand what the behavior is communicating.	❑ Not evident ❑ Emerging ❑ Evident ❑ Much evidence	Do teachers ask students what they need?
	Students are provided with an efficient communication system.	❑ Not evident ❑ Emerging ❑ Evident ❑ Much evidence	In what ways do students communicate in the classroom?
Classroom removal	Teachers do not remove students from the classroom in response to behavior.	❑ Not evident ❑ Emerging ❑ Evident ❑ Much evidence	How do the teachers respond?
	Students are encouraged to work through their problems with peers or adults.	❑ Not evident ❑ Emerging ❑ Evident ❑ Much evidence	What strategies do teachers employ to promote student independence?
Reinforcement	Teachers use reinforcements that are personally and socially valued and meaningful.	❑ Not evident ❑ Emerging ❑ Evident ❑ Much evidence	What reinforcements are used?
	Students have choice with their reinforcement.	❑ Not evident ❑ Emerging ❑ Evident ❑ Much evidence	How do students respond to reinforcements?

Figure 8.1.   Supporting Behavior Feedback Form.

(continued)

Figure 8.1.   *(continued)*   *(page 2 of 2)*

Preventing behavior	Teachers focus on preventing behaviors rather than reacting to them.	❑ Not evident ❑ Emerging ❑ Evident ❑ Much evidence	What strategies do teachers use to prevent behavior?
	Students are taught new behaviors.	❑ Not evident ❑ Emerging ❑ Evident ❑ Much evidence	What replacement behaviors are being taught?
Building relationships	Teachers have rapport with students.	❑ Not evident ❑ Emerging ❑ Evident ❑ Much evidence	Do teachers listen to students and do they have empathy?
	Students have friendships within the class and feel a sense of belonging.	❑ Not evident ❑ Emerging ❑ Evident ❑ Much evidence	What friendships exist and with whom do students interact?
Meeting students' instructional needs	Teachers use multiple intelligences theory in their instruction.	❑ Not evident ❑ Emerging ❑ Evident ❑ Much evidence	How are multiple intelligences reflected in instruction and assessment?
	Student interests and strengths are highlighted in instruction.	❑ Not evident ❑ Emerging ❑ Evident ❑ Much evidence	Are students involved in meaningful and interesting instruction that challenges them?
Additional considerations	How do teachers attempt to understand their students' needs? (In other words, do students need more joy in their school day? Do they need more choices and control? Do students need relationships? A sense of belonging? More autonomy? Access to communication?)		
	In what ways does the classroom environment promote positive behavior (e.g., student interaction, seating arrangements, structure through agendas, student work on walls)?		

Comments: _____

_____

_____

membership is contingent on being quiet or good. Of course the team wants to think about other students, but when inclusion is done well, all students understand that a certain student may make noise and that the student is working on that, just as other students may be working on other skills. Most students are surprisingly patient when given the chance and some information.

CONCLUSION

The way educators and paraprofessionals plan for, support, and react to behavior is critical to student success. The leadership of a principal is essential in helping all school team members to support students effectively. Figure 8.1 provides you with a form for giving feedback to teams about behavior. Remembering that all behavior communicates something and that all people need love and patience will help your teams be successful when supporting students. Supporting students who have challenging behavior is not easy; therefore, the next (and last) chapter of this book focuses on caring for yourself so that you can have the energy and ability to provide the best possible care for all students.

NOTES

9

Supporting You, Supporting Them

Caring for Yourself

KNOWING HOW HARD IT IS TO EFFECT
MEANINGFUL CHANGE IN PEOPLE,
MR. MOODY DECIDES TO
WORK HIS WAY UP TO IT BY
TEACHING OLD LOGS NEW TRICKS.

"Every day there are new stresses to maintaining an authentic inclusive school; the work is never done and neither is the resistance."

—*Meg (principal)*

"We know the principal sets the course for inclusion, but I also could not become a martyr. I needed to champion our inclusive direction and not run myself into the ground at the same time."

—*Jeff (principal)*

Many educators are perpetual students of the process called *self-care*. An ongoing part of their development is finding ways to nurture themselves—personally and professionally. As professors, authors, consultants and, most important, parents of two children, we too are often in real and continual need of self-care. In one memorable quest for self-care techniques, Julie found herself standing in the self-help aisle at the local bookstore with a close friend, reading different passages aloud. The books stated the reader should "become a bonsai tree" or "imagine myself on a glen surrounded by animals while breathing deeply." Julie's first thoughts were, "What is a glen?" and "What kind of animals?" "Are they dangerous?" "Are they rabid?" We began to laugh until other customers looked at us askance. At another moment of self-care reflection, George declared, "I know all this therapy is good for me, but I have to say I just need [a good friend], 45 minutes to run, then a bottle of wine." The point is that self-care is an ongoing process and one that requires attention.

Everyone takes care of himself or herself differently; every person needs to find the way that works best for him or her individually. This chapter does not provide you with a recipe for how to care for yourself; instead, it offers ideas or examples that may help you. Leaders who are not rested, healthy, and reasonably content will have difficulty running their schools. Whether you deal with stress by running a marathon or by taking a bath, it is important to focus on what you enjoy and on what works to help you relieve stress and feel healthy and balanced.

The job of a school leader is not easy. Then again, very few jobs worth doing are easy. We know that many principals find the job incredibly rewarding and incredibly stressful—varying day to day and even hour to hour. However, one thing is certain: you need to take care of yourself while taking care of others. We do not need school martyrs; we need school leaders. Just as we stated at the start this book, we know that the leader's role in inclusion is the most powerful predictor of success—so if you fall apart and cannot sustain your work in creating and maintaining an inclusive school, then all the stress and toil has been wasted.

In essence, you cannot give as fully to others, you cannot keep up the struggle of advocating for students with disabilities to be included fully and meaningfully, if you are not meeting your own needs. You cannot help others solve problems as well if you are overrun by your own stress. You need your own support system. This chapter begins with some strategies for problem solving. We then continue with lessons we have learned from school leaders committed to and engaged in this work of building inclusive schools about how they sustained themselves using professional strategies and self-care. This chapter (and book) concludes with a new job description for leadership.

PROBLEM SOLVING

Although you have read this book and have learned ideas and strategies to handle many different kinds of problems or situations, problems inevitably will arise that you may not feel prepared to handle. When you come across a problem that you are having difficulty solving, consider the following general ideas or suggestions (sometimes leaders forget that they do not need to have all the answers):

- Talk with teachers in your school.

- Bring the problem to the special education teachers.

- Talk with other leaders or other principals.

- List all the potential solutions.

- Talk to the student.

- Talk with the superintendent.

- Talk to a parent.

- Talk with a paraprofessional.

- Draw the problem.

- Go for a walk—think only of solutions during the walk.

- Talk to your best friend or partner (keep all information about students confidential).

If meeting with others or brainstorming solutions by yourself does not help you discover a new solution, you may need a step-by-step problem-solving process, such as creative problem-solving (CPS).

CREATIVE PROBLEM-SOLVING PROCESS

The CPS process has a long history as a proven method for approaching and solving problems in innovative ways (Davis, 2004; Parnes, 1985, 1988, 1992, 1997). It is a tool that can help you redefine a problem, come up with creative ways to solve the problem, and then take action to solve it. Julie originally learned this method and used it as a teacher to solve problems with the students she supported. Julie continues to use this method to solve everyday personal and professional problems. Alex Osborn and Sidney Parnes (Osborn, 1993) conducted extensive research on the steps involved when people solve problems. They determined that people typically use a five-step process. Each step is described in the following list.

Explore the Problem

1. *Fact finding*—Describe what you know or perceive to be true about the challenge. Who? What? When? Where? How? What is true and not true about this problem?

2. *Problem finding*—Clarify the issue. View it in a different way. Finish this sentence: In what ways might we . . .?

Generate Ideas

3. *Idea finding*—Generate as many ideas as possible; defer judgment and reinforcement (i.e., do not say things such as "good idea" or "that will not work," because then you would be passing judgment on the idea).

Prepare for Action

4. *Solution finding*—Compare the ideas against some criteria that you create. How will you know whether your solution will work? See Table 9.1 for sample criteria.

5. *Acceptance finding*—Create a step-by-step plan of action.

Table 9.1.   The creative problem-solving process in action

Stage of creative problem-solving process	Examples from Trevor's team
1. Fact finding	It doesn't work to wait him out.
	It takes easily 10 minutes to get him off the playground.
	He does not respond to everyone leaving the playground—he continues to play.
	He enjoys playing tag with his friends.
	He has trouble with transitions.
	No one has ever asked him what he needs.
2. Problem finding	In what ways can we help Trevor return from recess promptly and happily?
3. Idea finding	Give him a time-out.
	Have him lose minutes off his recess time.
	Give him a timer or watch.
	Have a peer help him in.
	See how long he will play outside before coming in.
	Don't allow him to go outside for recess at all.
	Make a sticker chart.
	Give him extra recess.

Stage of creative problem-solving process	Examples from Trevor's team
4. Solution finding	We want this solution to . . . (example criteria)
	1. Enhance the image of the student among peers
	2. Promote independence or interdependence
	3. Appeal to the student
	4. Increase and promote belonging
	5. Increase interaction with peers
	6. Seem logistically feasible
5. Acceptance finding	The team finally decided on a solution for this problem, combining three ideas. They first met with Trevor to ask him what would help (they provided him with a menu of ideas); he decided on a timer with peer support. They gave Trevor a watch timer and asked him to identify a peer whom he was to find when the timer went off. When the timer rang (with 2 minutes remaining in recess), the two boys found each other and went to line up together. Problem solved.

Sources: Giangreco, Cloninger, Dennis, and Edelman (2002); Osborn (1993).

The following example describes how this process actually worked in solving a specific problem for a paraprofessional.

• • • • • • •

Tom, a paraprofessional working with Trevor, a first-grade boy, was having a difficult time getting Trevor off the playground at the end of recess. Trevor would run around and hide, and Tom could not reach him or get him to go inside. The end of recess time was becoming a bit like a game of tag, except that Tom definitely did not enjoy chasing Trevor around. Trevor would climb to the top of the slide, and if Tom came up, Trevor would slide down. If Tom went up the slide, Trevor would go down the monkey bars. This was almost humorous to watch—unless you were Tom, who felt frustrated and embarrassed. Tom considered the communicative intent of the behavior and decided that Trevor was likely trying to communicate that he did not want to come in from recess. Knowing that information, however, did not help Tom identify what to do to get Trevor inside. He also knew that Trevor had a difficult time with transitions. Tom decided to talk to his team and the principal. Clearly, the principal could have joined Tom in chasing Trevor; the principal could have punished Trevor. Instead, they got the team together and engaged in a CPS process, which is briefly outlined in Table 9.1.

• • • • • • •

LESSONS FROM INCLUSIVE LEADERS: SUSTAINING THIS WORK

Sustaining inclusive leadership requires a combination of strategies. We have learned through a decade of research on this topic that principals require professional strategies to approach their work in different ways, as well as self-care strategies. The following section details these key lessons.

Professional Strategies

We define *professional strategies* as strategies leaders use in their jobs that both advance their work toward inclusive schooling and help sustain them personally. These professional strategies include the following:

- Communicating purposefully and authentically

- Developing a supportive administrator network

- Working together for change

- Engaging in professional learning

- Building relationships

Communicating Purposefully and Authentically   The first professional strategy that leaders use to advance inclusion in the face of resistance is communicating purposefully and authentically. Leaders tell us that, even if they do not make a particular change right away, they believe it necessary to communicate in a manner that rings true to their vision and values. This communication takes various forms, from asking the right questions to confronting a specific person to using humor. Using this purposeful and authentic communication creates some momentum in the direction of inclusion, reaffirms the belief in inclusion to those around them, and helps the leader feel that, even though a particular change may be slow, he or she did something by speaking truth. Sometimes this means asking the right question; other times, it means explaining the impact of a decision someone already made.

Developing a Supportive Administrator Network   Another essential strategy used by leaders committed to inclusive schooling involves developing a supportive network of administrators. These networks provide opportunities to share ideas, emotional support, encouragement, and assistance in problem solving. Principal Taylor describes the small network she has cultivated:

> I'm really using my colleagues as resources. I have a few people who really are on the same page as me about creating an authentic inclusive school . . . We can't just be out there on our own, so that has really made a big difference. . . . It's been huge and I think I'm finding myself calling people more often, taking the time to say, I need a minute, I need to bounce this off of somebody, I don't have to make this decision on my own.

Leaders striving for fully inclusive schools find that having colleagues they can talk with—colleagues who share similar ideals, colleagues they trust—creates the needed feeling of support. These leaders purposefully develop and use this network to advance their work, but perhaps more important, to sustain themselves. These networks help dissolve the sense of isolation and feelings of loneliness that accompany this hard work.

Working Together for Change   The next professional strategy that leaders of inclusive schools use to sustain their work involves empowering staff and community members as a strategy to advance inclusion in the face of significant pressures. Such leaders recognize that sharing decision making and empowering staff is a strategy that creates a sense of ownership in decisions, resulting in greater buy-in and, in turn, less pressure on the leader. The pressure that remains is then not directed solely at the leader; instead, the group shares it. As part of this process of working together, leaders learn to delegate and trust other staff. They figure out what work can wait and what they need to accomplish in order to keep their jobs and also sleep at night. One principal summarized the essence of this strategy: "Over and over I had to evaluate, what is possible now, what can wait, what can I give to someone else, and what do I personally need to do to not go crazy." As leaders of inclusive schools work with others for change, they also prioritize their work.

Engaging in Professional Learning   The next professional strategy involves engaging in professional learning. "I like to read, I like to learn about what people are doing to make things right." This strategy, expressed by Principal Natalie, typified the learning priority that she and others share. Ongoing learning helps leaders better accomplish their agenda in the face of significant barriers. One principal stated, "The book study groups, the learning we do as a staff, really helped me with some of the stress I feel as far as reducing my questioning myself about, am I competent to do this?"

Building Relationships   The last professional strategy leaders report using to advance inclusion in the face of resistance involves building relationships. Principal Tracy explained how important he believes relationships are:

> I spent a lot of time building relationships with families and students and staff. I became incredibly purposeful about it. I think in a way that really helped ease the struggle . . . it becomes much easier to work with challenging kids if you've built a relationship, if you know them and if they like you . . . Even staff who might disagree with a particular idea or initiative felt "I don't like the idea, but I know Tracy cares so much about our kids, I can accept this because I trust him, I know he is being sincere". . . . It also makes the day much more fun, it makes the job more enjoyable. You feel like a part of a community so I think personal relationships definitely are a strategy. At first I thought it [building relationships] was my job, but it also became very helpful in terms of my emotional well-being.

Self-Care

Have you ever been on an airplane and heard a flight attendant announce that, if there is an emergency, you should place an oxygen mask on your own face before assisting your children? The idea behind that rule is that, if the plane crashes, you want to make sure you are available to help the children. If you do not have oxygen, you will not be able to help them. In essence, that is what self-care involves: nurturing yourself outside of work so that you can be helpful and nurturing to the school, staff, and children in your care.

Maslow (1999) identified the basic physiological needs of every human; these include oxygen, food, water, and regulated body temperature. Like any other human being, you need to make sure your needs are being met before you can help meet the needs of others. You might have to bring healthy snacks to school to keep yourself fueled for a long day at work. You might bring a water bottle with you so that you can stay hydrated throughout the day. Maslow's next level of need is safety and love. Surround yourself with loving people so that you feel loved and supported. Last, you need to get enough sleep every night. It is much more difficult to be prepared to support your staff if you are tired and cranky. These needs are at the very core of every person's physical and mental health.

Next we describe self-care strategies we have seen that allow leaders to maintain their individual sanity in order to continue their inclusive work. These strategies are distinct from the professional ones described previously, in that they are not about the leader rethinking the daily work, but rather about keeping themselves going and emotionally fit. We identify four productive self-care strategies we see leaders use and one less productive one:

- Prioritizing life outside school

- Utilizing mindful diversions

- Engaging in regular physical activity

- Providing for others

- Employing potentially harmful behaviors

Prioritizing Life Outside School The first self-care strategy is purposefully setting aside time to leave work and school behind. Principal Meg says this strategy helps her by "feeding myself with friendships, the same kind of people who care about the same thing." She continued this sentiment about her family:

> I'm purposeful about not cutting time out of my own kids' time. I keep the job between . . . whenever I leave in the morning, whether that's 5:30 or 7:15 [a.m.]. The job ends for me at the latest at 5:00 in the evening and I don't think I've violated that at all. . . . Very seldom is there any exception to that, in terms of crowding out my own kids' time.

We see that consciously making time or drawing time boundaries for life outside of school helps principals maintain an essential connection to people important in their lives and also helps keep the pressures and huge responsibilities at bay.

Utilizing Mindful Diversions The second self-care strategy involves taking part in activities for your own enjoyment for the purpose of getting away from the pressures of work. These can clear the mind of at least some of the stress and turmoil brought from school. Principal Tracy describes a diversion that helps him:

We have people over for dinner a lot, I really love to cook, and cooking is a great stress-relief strategy for me. For some reason when I cook I don't think about all the stress of school. So, even though it adds an extra layer of work, an extra thing to do, it gives me some peace. . . . [It is] probably the thing which most helps me keep my sanity.

Remembering to add diversions brings a certain level of fun and enjoyment and allows leaders the opportunity to clear their minds.

Engaging in Regular Physical Activity

The next self-care strategy we identified involves leaders keeping their bodies in strong enough shape to maintain the hectic pace and resist the immense pressure they face. Principal Eli states:

I exercise, I think physical exercise is really important . . . it takes some getting used to, but you've got to find time to exercise. The best time for me is 5:00 in the morning, so almost every day I get up early . . . the running is great for me physically and mentally. I've got a group of people I run with, and that helps, too.

Providing for Others

It is important to note that providing for others outside of school can be an effective self-care strategy. The combination of accomplishing something tangible and the feeling of helping someone else that is not related to the school is a self-care strategy we have seen leaders use. Principal Natalie explains, "I take care of my neighbors. . . . We mow lawns for them, we make sure that they have what they need, I help them clean up their house and yard . . . those things make me feel like I'm doing something tangible."

> **EMPLOYING POTENTIALLY HARMFUL BEHAVIORS:** We recognize that a number of leaders, in the face of significant resistance to inclusion, employ potentially harmful behaviors (e.g., overworking, increasing alcohol consumption, trying to do the work alone). It is not our intent to judge school leaders, nor are we endorsing potentially harmful strategies. We do feel an obligation to share the strategies we see that may seem to help in the relative short-term but contain dangerous long-term effects. Whatever you do, try to keep your solutions for self-care positive and constructive. We recognize that there are other strategies outside of those discussed here (therapy, goal setting, scheduled time off, etc.). We recommend purposeful effort in finding those that work for you (the reader) and recognizing that this is ongoing and lifelong work.

Find an Outlet

Caring for yourself is critical to staying on the job and feeling balanced while doing it. Whether you use professional strategies or self-care, we encourage you to find ways to sustain yourself both at and outside of work. Build networks of support at your school and in your personal lives. Consider physical outlets such as yoga, running, walking, biking, hiking, or swimming. Consider spiritual outlets such as meditation, prayer, or yoga to keep yourself spiritually balanced.

You may want to turn to intellectual outlets such as playing games, reading, or writing. Or, try creative outlets such as painting, sculpting, drawing, baking, cooking, making scrapbooks, or generally creating something. Consider engaging in self-pampering activities such as taking baths or getting massages. Employing these types of self-care strategies will help you feel balanced, healthy, and calm. See the Chapter 9 Appendix for a list of books on self-care. Everyone needs professional and personal care, and we encourage you to use some of these strategies to think about and engage in your own self-care.

As we have mentioned, we consider ourselves learners, especially in the area of self-care. When working in schools and being responsible for the education of many children, educators need to be constantly learning from them and for them. Our hope is that this book will be an impetus for your own learning. After reading this book, try out the strategies, and when you identify a strategy or idea that works, use it again. At the same time, remember that every context, every student, and every minute brings something new. It is important to reflect on when certain ideas or strategies work and how they work. The process is inevitably fluid. At the end of each day, ask yourself the following questions: 1) What worked today? 2) What did not work? 3) What do I want to do differently tomorrow?

We conclude this book with a new job description for school leaders—a call to do things differently. We thank you for reading, and we wish you luck as you create and maintain inclusive schools in order to help students to reach their full academic and social potential.

HOW TO REALLY CREATE AND SUPPORT AN INCLUSIVE SCHOOL: A NEW LEADERSHIP JOB DESCRIPTION

Know yourself. Have a vision. Include each and every child. Listen to your students. Listen to your staff. Listen to your families. Watch them. Hear them. Learn from them. Set an inclusive direction. Be bold. Be humble.

Foster belonging for each student; for each member of your staff; for each family. Be there, but give them space. Be warm. Be demanding. Expect everyone to learn. Expect some risks. Let them fail sometimes. Encourage independence. Love them all. Stop yelling. Handle people with care. Be respectful. Be gentle. Be out in front. Question inequity. Do what you say you will.

Ask, "What do you need?" "How can we include this student?" "What do we need to get better?" "How can I best help you?" "What should be celebrated?" "Who are we serving well?" "Who aren't we serving well?"

Remember, children with disabilities are people first.

Have lots of tissues. If students are sad, wipe their tears. If staff members are sad, listen and support. Help students connect. Help staff build teams. Assume friendship is possible. Assume collaboration is possible. Allow students to create together, laugh together, have fun together. Allow staff to create together, think together, argue together, have fun together. Encourage interdependence. Assume competence always. Attribute the best possible motive consistent with the facts. Spark curiosity. Set high expectations. Do not control. Confront injustice.

When students are happy, step back. When staff members are happy, celebrate. When families are happy, celebrate! Relax. Be a learner yourself. Share positive stories about students, staff, and families. Set students up to be successful. Create conditions for all to thrive together. Build opportunities for families to partner, and not just those people who usually show up.

When students have difficulties, kindly redirect. Breathe. Engage. Expect great things from everyone. Speak softly. Encourage softly. Redirect softly. Lead by loving. Watch them thrive. Be bold. Include everyone—each and every one.

NOTES

9
Appendix

SELF-CARE BOOKS

Byrne, R. (2006). *The secret*. New York, NY: Atria Books/Beyond Words.

Carlson, R. (1998). *Don't sweat the small stuff at work: Simple ways to minimize stress and conflict while bringing out the best in yourself and others*. New York, NY: Hyperion.

Covey, S.R. (2004). *The 7 habits of highly effective people: Powerful lessons in personal change* (15th anniversary ed.). New York, NY: Free Press.

Fontana, D. (1999). *Learn to meditate: A practical guide to self-discovery*. London, United Kingdom: Duncan Baird.

Hoff, B. (1983). *The tao of Pooh*. New York, NY: Penguin.

Moran, V. (1999). *Creating a charmed life: Sensible, spiritual secrets every busy woman should know*. New York, NY: HarperOne.

Palmer, P. (1999). *Let your life speak: Listening to the voice of vocation*. San Francisco, CA: Jossey-Bass.

Palmer, P. (2004). *A hidden wholeness: The journey towards the undivided life*. San Francisco, CA: Jossey-Bass.

Reynolds, S. (2005). *Better than chocolate*. Berkeley, CA: Ten Speed Press.

SARK. (1991). *A creative companion: How to free your creative spirit*. New York, NY: Fireside.

SARK. (1994). *Living juicy: Daily morsels for your creative soul*. New York, NY: Fireside.

SARK. (1997). *Succulent wild women*. New York, NY: Fireside.

SARK. (2005). *Make your creative dreams real: A plan for procrastinators, perfectionists, busy people, and people who would really rather sleep all day*. New York, NY: Fireside.

Topchik, G. (2001). *Managing workplace negativity*. New York, NY: AMACOM.

Wheatley, M.J. (2002). *Turning to one another: Simple conversation to restore hope in the future*. San Francisco, CA: Berrett-Koehler Press.

References

American Psychiatric Association. (2000). *Diagnostic and statistical manual of mental disorders* (4th ed., text revision). Washington, DC: Author.

Armstrong, T. (2000a). *In their own way: Discovering and encouraging your child's multiple intelligences.* New York, NY: Jeremy P. Tarcher, Penguin Group (USA) LLC.

Armstrong, T. (2000b). *Multiple intelligences in the classroom.* Alexandria, VA: Association for Supervision and Curriculum Development.

Ashby, C.E. (2008). *"Cast into a cold pool": Inclusion and access in middle school for students with labels of mental retardation and autism* (Unpublished doctoral dissertation). Syracuse University, Syracuse, NY.

Barger-Anderson, R., Isherwood, R.S., & Merhaut, J. (2013). *Strategic co-teaching in your school: Using the co-design model.* Baltimore, MD: Paul H. Brookes Publishing Co.

Battle, D. (2009). *Characteristics of public, private, and Bureau of Indian Education elementary and secondary school principals in the United States: Results from the 2007–08 Schools and Staffing Survey.* Washington, DC: National Center for Education Statistics.

Bedingfield, S. (Producer), & Wurtzburg, G. (Director). (2004). *Autism is a world* [Motion picture]. United States: CNN.

Biklen, D. (2005). Framing autism. In D. Biklen (with A. Attfield, L. Bissonnette, L. Blackman, J. Burke, A. Frugone, T. Rajarshi Mukhopadhyay, & S. Rubin), *Autism and the myth of the person alone* (pp. 80–82). New York, NY: New York University Press.

Biklen, D. (Producer), & Wurtzburg, G. (Director). (2011). *Wretches & jabberers* [Motion picture]. United States: Gravitas Ventures.

Biklen, D., & Burke, J. (2006). Presuming competence. *Equity and Excellence in Education, 39,* 166–175.

Blatt, B. (1987). *The conquest of mental retardation.* Austin, TX: PRO-ED.

Bonner Foundation. (2008). Conflict resolution: Steps for handling interpersonal dynamics. In *Bonner civic engagement training modules.* Retrieved from http://bonnernetwork.pbworks.com/w/page/13112080/Bonner%20Training%20Modules%20%28with%20Descriptions%29

Byrne, R. (2006). *The secret.* New York, NY: Atria Books/Beyond Words.

Callahan, C. (1997). *Advice about being an LD student.* Retrieved from http://www.ldonline.org/firstperson/8550

Capper, C.A., & Frattura, E. (2008). *Meeting the needs of students of all abilities: How leaders go beyond inclusion* (2nd ed.). Thousand Oaks, CA: Corwin Press.

Capper, C.A., Frattura, E., & Keyes, M.W. (2000). *Meeting the needs of students of all abilities: How leaders go beyond inclusion.* Thousand Oaks, CA: Corwin Press.

Carlson, R. (1998). *Don't sweat the small stuff at work: Simple ways to minimize stress and conflict while bringing out the best in yourself and others.* New York, NY: Hyperion.

Carr, E.G., Dunlap, G., Horner, R.H., Koegel, R.L., Turnbull, A., Sailor, W., …, Fox, L. (2002). Positive behavior support: Evolution of an applied science. *Journal of Positive Behavior Interventions, 4*(1), 4–16.

Casey, K., & Vanceburg, M. (1996). *A promise of a new day: A book of daily meditations.* Center City, MN: Hazelden.

Causton-Theoharis, J. (2003). *Increasing interactions between students with disabilities and their peers via paraprofessional training* (Unpublished doctoral dissertation). University of Wisconsin–Madison.

Causton-Theoharis, J. (2009). *The paraprofessional's handbook for effective support in inclusive classrooms.* Baltimore, MD: Paul H. Brookes Publishing Co.

Causton-Theoharis, J., & Theoharis, G. (2008, September). Creating inclusive schools for all students. *The School Administrator, 65*(8), 24–30.

Cosier, M. (2010). *Exploring the relationship between inclusive education and achievement: New perspectives* (Unpublished doctoral dissertation). Syracuse University, Syracuse, NY.

Cosier, M., Causton-Theoharis, J., & Theoharis, G. (2013). Does access matter? Time in general education and achievement for students with disabilities. *Remedial and Special Education.*

Covey, S.R. (2004). *The 7 habits of highly effective people: Powerful lessons in personal change* (15th anniversary ed.). New York, NY: Free Press.

Data Accountability Center. (2010). *Individuals with disabilities education act (IDEA) data. Part B data & notes.* Retrieved on May 12, 2012 from https://www.ideadata.org/PartBData.asp

Davis, G. (2004). *Creativity is forever* (5th ed.). Dubuque, IA: Kendall Hunt.

Donnellan, A. (1984). The criterion of the least dangerous assumption. *Behavioral Disorders, 9,* 141–150.

Doyle, M.B. (2008). *The paraprofessional's guide to the inclusive classroom: Working as a team* (3rd ed.). Baltimore, MD: Paul H. Brookes Publishing Co.

Edmonds, R. (1979). Effective schools for the urban poor. *Educational Leadership, 37*(1), 15–24.

Education for All Handicapped Children Act of 1975, PL 94–142, 20 U.S.C. §§ 1400 *et seq.*

FAS Community Resource Center. (2008). *Information about fetal alcohol syndrome (FAS) and fetal alcohol spectrum disorders (FASD).* Retrieved from http://www.come-over.to/FAS/fasprint.htm

Ferri, B.A. (2011). Undermining inclusion? A critical reading of response to intervention (RTI). *International Journal of Inclusive Education.* doi: 10.1080/13603116.2010.538862

Fontana, D. (1999). *Learn to meditate: A practical guide to self-discovery.* London, United Kingdom: Duncan Baird.

Frattura, E., & Capper, C.A. (2007). *Leading for social justice: Transforming schools for all learners.* Thousand Oaks, CA: Corwin Press.

Friend, M. (2005). *The Power of 2* [DVD]. Available from www.forumoneducation.org

Friend, M., & Bursuck, W.D. (2011). *Including students with special needs: A practical guide for classroom teachers.* Boston, MA: Pearson Education.

Friend, M., & Cook, L. (2006). *Interactions: Collaboration skills for school professionals* (4th ed.). Boston, MA: Allyn & Bacon

Friend, M., & Reising, M. (1993, Summer). Co-teaching: An overview of the past, a glimpse at the present, and considerations for the future. *Preventing School Failure, 37*(4), 6–10.

Gabel, A. (2006). Stop asking me if I need help. In E.B. Keefe, V.M. Moore, & F.R. Duff (Eds.), *Listening to the experts: Students with disabilities speak out* (pp. 35–40). Baltimore, MD: Paul H. Brookes Publishing Co.

Gardner, H. (1993). *Frames of mind: A theory of multiple intelligences.* New York, NY: Basic Books.

Giangreco, M.F., Cloninger, C.J., Dennis, R., & Edelman, S.W. (2002). Problem-solving methods to facilitate inclusive education. In J.S. Thousand, R.A. Villa, & A.I. Nevin (Eds.), *Creativity and collaborative learning: The practical guide to empowering students, teachers, and families* (2nd ed., pp. 111–134). Baltimore, MD: Paul H. Brookes Publishing Co.

Habib, D. (Producer, Director). (2008). *Including Samuel* [Motion picture]. United States: DH Institute on Disability/UCED.

Hoff, B. (1983). *The tao of Pooh.* New York, NY: Penguin.

Huefner, D.S. (2000). *Getting comfortable with special education law: A framework for working with children with disabilities.* Norwood, MA: Christopher-Gordon.

Individuals with Disabilities Education Improvement Act (IDEA) of 2004, PL 108–446, 20 U.S.C. §§ 1400 *et seq.*

Information on bipolar and other mental health disorders. (n.d.) *Borderline personality disorder.* Retrieved from http://www.angelfire.com/home/bphoenix1/border.html

Institut Pasteur. (n.d.). *Louis Pasteur's biography.* Retrieved from http://www.pasteur.fr/ip/easysite/pasteur/fr/institut-pasteur/histoire/biographie-de-louis-pasteur#

Janney, R., & Snell, M.E. (2008). *Teachers' guides to inclusive practices: Behavioral support* (2nd ed.). Baltimore, MD: Paul H. Brookes Publishing Co.

Kafka, J. (2009). The principalship in historical perspective. *Peabody Journal of Education, 84,* 318–320.

Keller, H. (1903). *The story of my life.* New York, NY: Doubleday, Page.

Kinney, P. (2003). Leading with less. *Principal, 83*(1), 34–35, 38–39.

Kliewer, C., & Biklen, D. (1996). Labeling: Who wants to be called retarded? In W. Stainback & S. Stainback (Eds.), *Controversial issues confronting special education: Divergent perspectives* (2nd ed., pp. 83–111). Boston, MA: Allyn & Bacon.

Kluth, P. (2003). *"You're going to love this kid!" Teaching students with autism in the inclusive classroom.* Baltimore, MD: Paul H. Brookes Publishing Co.

Kluth, P. (2005). Calm in crisis. Adapted from P. Kluth (2003), *"You're going to love this kid!" Teaching students with autism in the inclusive classroom.* Baltimore, MD: Paul H. Brookes Publishing Co. Retrieved from http://www.paulakluth.com/readings/autism/calm-in-crisis/

Kluth, P., & Dimon-Borowski, M. (2003). *Strengths and strategies profile.* Retrieved from http://www.paulakluth.com/wordpress/wp-content/uploads/2011/03/strengthstrategy.pdf

Knoster, T.P. (2008). *The teacher's pocket guide for effective classroom management.* Baltimore, MD: Paul H. Brookes Publishing Co.

Kohn, A. (2006). *Beyond discipline: From compliance to community* (10th anniversary ed.). Alexandria, VA: Association for Supervision and Curriculum Development.

Kornhaber, M., Fierros, E., & Veenema, S. (2004). *Multiple intelligences: Best ideas from research and practice.* Boston, MA: Pearson Education.

Kunc, N. (1992). The need to belong: Rediscovering Maslow's hierarchy of needs. In R. Villa, J. Thousand, W. Stainback, & S. Stainback (Eds.), *Restructuring for caring and effective education* (pp. 21–40). Baltimore, MD: Paul H. Brookes Publishing Co.

Langer, S., & Boris-Schacter, S. (2003). Challenging the image of the American principalship. *Principal, 83*(1), 14–18.

Latham, G.I. (1999). *Parenting with love: Making a difference in a day.* Logan, UT: P&T Ink.

Living with ADD. (2004). *Brian.* Retrieved from http://livingwithadd.com/profiles/blogs/brian-s-story-1

Lovett, H. (1996). *Learning to listen: Positive approaches and people with difficult behavior.* Baltimore, MD: Paul H. Brookes Publishing Co.

Manasse, A.L. (1985). Improving conditions for principal effectiveness: Policy implications of research. *The Elementary School Journal, 85*(3), 138–162.

Marshall, C. (2004). Social justice challenges to educational administration: Introduction to a special issue. *Educational Administration Quarterly, 40*(1), 5–15.

Maslow, A.H. (1999). *Toward a psychology of being.* New York, NY: John Wiley & Sons.

Mavis. (2003, October 7). *Living in the hearing and deaf worlds.* Retrieved from http://www.raisingdeafkids.org/meet/deaf/mavis/worlds.php

McLeskey, J., & Waldron, N.L. (2002). School change and inclusive schools: Lessons learned from practice. *Phi Delta Kappan, 84*(1), 65–72.

McLeskey, J., & Waldron, N. (2006). Comprehensive school reform and inclusive schools: Improving schools for all students. *Theory into Practice, 45*(3), 269–278.

Molton, K. (2000). *Dispelling some myths about autism.* Retrieved from http://www.autism.org.uk/about-autism/myths-facts-and-statistics/myths-and-facts.aspx

Moran, V. (1999). *Creating a charmed life: Sensible, spiritual secrets every busy woman should know.* New York, NY: HarperOne.

Murawski, W.W., & Dieker, L.A. (2004). Tips and strategies for co-teaching at the secondary level. *TEACHING Exceptional Children, 36*(5), 52–58.

National Center for Education Statistics. (2011). *Children 3 to 21 years old served in federally supported programs for the disabled, by type of disability: Selected years, 1976–77 through 2009–10.* Retrieved from http://nces.ed.gov/fastfacts/display.asp?id=64

No Child Left Behind Act of 2001, PL 107–110, 115 Stat. 1425, 20 U.S.C. §§ 6301 *et seq.*

Orwell, G. (1946). Politics and the English language. *Horizon, 13*(76), 252–265. Retrieved from https://www.mtholyoke.edu/acad/intrel/orwell46.htm

Osborn, A.F. (1993). *Applied imagination: Principles and procedures of creative problem-solving* (3rd rev. ed.). Buffalo, NY: Creative Education Foundation Press. (Original work published 1953)

Palmer, P. (1999). *Let your life speak: Listening to the voice of vocation.* San Francisco, CA: Jossey-Bass.

Palmer, P. (2004). *A hidden wholeness: The journey towards the undivided life.* San Francisco, CA: Jossey-Bass.

Parker, K. (2008). *Meet RhapsodyBlue.* Retrieved from http://www.angelfire.com/country/rhapsody blue22/page2.html

Parnes, S.J. (1985). *A facilitating style of leadership.* Buffalo, NY: Bearly.

Parnes, S.J. (1988). *Visionizing: State-of-the-art processes for encouraging innovative excellence.* East Aurora, NY: D.O.K. Publishing.

Parnes, S.J. (Ed.). (1992). *Source book for creative problem solving: A fifty-year digest of proven innovation processes.* Buffalo, NY: Creative Education Foundation Press.

Parnes, S.J. (1997). *Optimize the magic of your mind.* Buffalo, NY: Creative Education Foundation Press.

Paul-Brown, D., & Diggs, M.C. (1993, Winter). Recognizing and treating speech and language disabilities. *American Rehabilitation, 19*(4), 30.

Pazey, B.L., & Cole, H.A. (2013). The role of special education training in the development of socially just leaders: Building an equity consciousness in educational leadership programs. *Educational Administration Quarterly, 29*(2), 243–271.

PEAK Parent Center. (n.d.). *Accommodations and modifications fact sheet.* Retrieved from http://www.peatc.org/peakaccom.htm

Pearpoint, J., O'Brien, J., & Forest, M. (1993). *PATH (Planning Alternative Tomorrows with Hope): A workbook for planning positive futures.* Toronto, Canada: Inclusion Press.

Peterson, J.M., & Hittie, M.M. (2002). *Inclusive teaching: Creating effective schools for all children.* Boston, MA: Allyn & Bacon.

Peterson, J.M., & Hittie, M.M. (2009). *Inclusive teaching: The journey toward effective schools for all children.* Boston, MA: Allyn & Bacon.

Pitonyak, D. (2010). *The importance of belonging.* Retrieved from http://www.dimagine.com/Belonging.pdf

Reynolds, S. (2005). *Better than chocolate.* Berkeley, CA: Ten Speed Press.

Riehl, C.J. (2000). The principal's role in creating inclusive schools for diverse students: A review of normative, empirical, and critical literature on the practice of educational administration. *Review of Educational Research, 70*(1), 55–81.

Rosa's Law, 2010, PL 111-256.

Rousmaniere, K. (2009). The great divide: Principals, teachers, and the long hallway between them. *History of Education Review, 38*(2), 17–27.

Rubin, S. (2003, December). *Making dreams come true.* Paper presented at the annual conference of TASH, Chicago, IL.

SARK. (1991). *A creative companion: How to free your creative spirit.* New York, NY: Fireside.

SARK. (1994). *Living juicy: Daily morsels for your creative soul.* New York, NY: Fireside.

SARK. (1997). *Succulent wild women.* New York, NY: Fireside.

SARK. (2005). *Make your creative dreams real: A plan for procrastinators, perfectionists, busy people, and people who would really rather sleep all day.* New York, NY: Fireside.

Schalock, R.L., & Braddock, D.L. (2002). *Out of the darkness and into the light: Nebraska's experience with mental retardation.* Washington, DC: American Association on Mental Retardation.

Shields, C.M., Larocque, L.J., & Oberg, S.L. (2002). A dialogue about race and ethnicity in education: Struggling to understand issues in cross-cultural leadership. *Journal of School Leadership, 12*(2), 116–137.

Snell, M., & Janney, R. (2005). *Teachers' guides to inclusive practices: Collaborative teaming* (2nd ed.). Baltimore, MD: Paul H. Brookes Publishing Co.

Snow, K. (2008). *To ensure inclusion, freedom, and respect for all, it's time to embrace people first language.* Retrieved from http://www.disabilityisnatural.com/explore/people-first-language

Strachan, J. (1997). *Resistance, agreement, and appropriation: Practicing feminist educational leadership in a "new right" context.* Paper presented at the general meeting of the American Educational Research Association, Chicago, IL.

Strully, J.L., & Strully, C. (1996). Friendships as an educational goal: What we have learned and where we are headed. In S. Stainback & W. Stainback (Eds.), *Inclusion: A guide for educators* (pp. 141–154). Baltimore, MD: Paul H. Brookes Publishing Co.

Taylor, R.L., Smiley, L.R., & Richards, S.B. (2009). *Exceptional students: Preparing teaching for the 21st century.* New York, NY: McGraw-Hill.

Theoharis, G. (2009).*The leadership our children deserve: 7 keys to equity, social justice, and school reform.* New York, NY: Teachers College Press.

Topchik, G. (2001). *Managing workplace negativity.* New York, NY: AMACOM.

Turnbull, H.R., Turnbull, A.R., Shank, M., & Smith, S.J. (2004). *Exceptional lives: Special education in today's schools* (4th ed.). Upper Saddle River, NJ: Merrill/Prentice Hall.

Udvari-Solner, A. (1997). Inclusive education. In C.A. Grant & G. Ladson-Billings (Eds.), *Dictionary of multicultural education* (pp. 141–144). Phoenix, AZ: Oryx Press.

U.S. Department of Education. (2004). *Twenty-fourth annual report to Congress on the implementation of the Individuals with Disabilities Education Act.* Washington, DC: Author.

U.S. Department of Education. (2007, September). *Twenty-seventh annual report to Congress on the implementation of the Individuals with Disabilities Education Act, 2005* (Vol. 1). Washington, DC: Author.

U.S. Department of Education, Office of Special Education and Rehabilitative Services, Office of Special Education Programs. (2009). *Twenty-eighth annual report to Congress on the implementation of the Individuals with Disabilities Education Act, 2006* (Vol. 1). Washington, DC: Author.

Villa, R., Thousand, J., Meyers, H., & Nevin, A. (1996). Teacher and administrator perceptions of heterogeneous education. *Exceptional Children, 63*(1), 29–45.

Villa, R., Thousand, J., & Nevin, A. (2008). *A guide to co-teaching: A multimedia kit for professional development* [multimedia]. Thousand Oaks, CA: Corwin Press.

Weil, S. (2001). *The need for roots.* London, United Kingdom: Routledge.

Wheatley, M.J. (2002). *Turning to one another: Simple conversation to restore hope in the future.* San Francisco, CA: Berrett-Koehler Press.

Williams, R. (Presenter/Interviewer), & Thompson, S. (Interviewee). (2008, August 24). Hearing impairment: A personal story [Radio series episode]. In Seega, B. (Executive Producer), *Ockham's razor.* Sydney, Australia: ABC Radio National. Retrieved from http://www.abc.net.au/rn/ockhams-razor/stories/2008/2342555.htm

Index

Page numbers followed by *b*, *f*, and *t* indicate boxes, figures, and tables, respectively.

The Paraprofessional's Handbook for Effective Support in Inclusive Classrooms

By Julie Causton-Theoharis, Ph.D.

"The best and most comprehensive information about the roles, responsibilities, and values of paraprofessionals."
—Lou Brown, Ph.D., Professor Emeritus, University of Wisconsin

"A book that everyone associated with inclusive education will want to read and talk about."
—Douglas Biklen, Dean of Education, Syracuse University

US$29.95 | Stock Number: BA-68998
2009 | 144 pages | 7 x 10 | paperback
ISBN 978-1-55766-899-8

What does a great paraprofessional need to know and do? Find out in this handy survival guide, equally useful for the brand-new paraprofessional or the 20-year classroom veteran. Packed with friendly guidance, practical tips, and first-person stories, this book reveals the best ways to provide effective services to students in inclusive classrooms.

Paraprofessionals will discover how to

- provide skillful and subtle support to students while encouraging their independence
- resolve challenging behavior in gentle and positive ways
- make informed decisions about content-specific accommodations and adaptations
- presume competence and keep expectations high
- facilitate peer supports and friendships
- partner with teachers, SLPs, families, and other members of the educational team
- believe their own stress and avoid burnout

The essential guide for every paraprofessional—and a must-have for the educators and other professionals who support them—this empowering book takes the guesswork out of a critical classroom role and helps students with disabilities reach their full potential.